Sex Positions:

14 Sex Ebooks in 1!!! Your Guide to Hundreds of Sex and Love Techniques, from Kama Sutra to Tantric Sex, Sexting Tips, Dirty Talk, and BDSM!!!

CW00952445

Sex Positions:

Your Guide to the 50 Best Sex Positions for a sexy marriage!

Contents

Introduction

I want to thank you and congratulate you for downloading the book, *"Sex Positions: Your Guide to the 50 Best Sex Positions for a sexy marriage!"*

This book contains proven steps and strategies on how to develop a more meaningful, satisfying, and lasting relationship with your spouse through sex.

Every couple goes through a honeymoon period where they just can't seem to take their hands off each other. But as other aspects of the relationship grow more important, couples begin to realize changes in their sexual appetites. When one of you suddenly wants to make love less than the other, this leads to bitterness and disillusionment.

A waning libido is a common problem among couples who have been sleeping with each other for years and years. Contrary to what most might think, it's not just because you no longer find your partner attractive. Often, it's because *you* no longer find *yourself* attractive. When you look into the mirror, cringe, and decide that even *you* wouldn't sleep with you, this destroys your self-esteem. And in order to feel aroused, you need to feel that you are desired and that you're worthy of being wanted. Through this book, you'll find tips on how to be sexy in the bedroom. You'll learn that feeling sexy and having great sex is not about defying the sands of time. It's about getting the years to work *for* you instead of *against* you.

Sex and stagnancy don't mix. Couples who make a continuous effort to re-explore each other's bodies and find new ways to please each other are bound to last longer than those who don't. In this book, you'll find 50 of the best sex positions ranging from positions that can give her multiple orgasms to positions that can make him feel like the ultimate alpha male between the sheets.

Thanks again for downloading this book, I hope you enjoy it!

Chapter 1

Sex and Successful Relationships

> ➢ **Sex connects you.**

And not just physically but mentally and emotionally as well. Most couples will agree that nothing can make you feel closer to your partner than when you're making love with him/her. The mere act of being naked together makes you vulnerable to each other. Thus, the act of lovemaking fosters feelings of trust and acceptance. When sex is a satisfactory experience, you both feel a sense of security in each other's arms. After sex, the feel-good hormone oxytocin is released into your bloodstream. This provides you both with a sense of calm and contentment, therefore enabling you to bond with each other.

> ➢ **Sex makes your relationship smoother.**

When couples who have been together for a long time start to neglect each other in the bedroom, this creates a strain on the relationship. The effects tend to manifest themselves gradually though insecurities, irritability, and impatience. Even your partner's tiny quirks become the subject of heated discussions. Before you know it, you are subconsciously doubting and resenting each other. The worst thing is you don't even know where all these negative emotions are coming from, only that you're feeling them.

On the other hand, couples who have sex regularly are more easygoing and tolerant of each other's flaws. They are better able to sail smoothly through the daily trials they encounter in their relationship. Sex is a great stress-reliever and coming home after a hard day's work and getting some O's immediately pushes your buttons to love mode instead of battle mode. Furthermore, getting more O's can help you get better Zzz's and a great night's sleep leads to a fight-free morning. Couples find that once they get into fixing their bedroom issues, other issues in their marriage just sort of work themselves out.

> ➢ **Sex enables you to communicate with each other.**

When you're married or dating each other exclusively, sex is a language of love which you don't get to share with anyone else apart from your partner. There are some messages that are best expressed through touch and when you have sex with your spouse/lover, you tell him/her: *"I love you."*, *"I need you."*, and *"I want to be with you."*

Some couples think that as the sands of time screws up their libido, it becomes a message that it's time to start lying low. On the contrary, sex in marriage or in any long-term relationship doesn't have an expiration date. In fact, being together for so long gives you more excuses to get between the sheets more often. Why? Because your partner is that one person in this world who understands your body like no one else can. He/she has seen, touched, and loved every bit of you. Your long-time lover knows what makes you tick. He/she knows what makes you go wild and soft, what makes you feel alive, and what makes you feel loved. Each time you make love, you remind each other why you belong with each other and why no one else will do.

> ## Sex helps you to build each other up.

When you have sex, you tell your partner how much you value him/her. The mere act of initiating sex reassures your partner that you still find him/her attractive after all these years. When you show interest in each other, you boost each other's egos. When you offer yourselves to each other and marvel in its each other's bodies, it sends these messages: *"I'm happy to be yours."* and *"I'm proud that you're mine."*

> ## Having sex more often keeps thoughts of infidelities away.

If you start neglecting your partner, this negatively affects his/her self-esteem. This makes your spouse/lover wonder about the causes of your waning affection. Once a seed of doubt has been planted, there's no stopping its evil branches from growing. Her/his speculations may range from *"He's having an affair."* to *"She doesn't love me anymore."*

Furthermore, such undesirable thoughts can push either one of you to seek happiness, comfort, and pleasure somewhere else. This can lead you to explore dangerous what ifs and what-might-have-beens (example: *"What if I'd married my ex instead, maybe I would've been happier."* or *"I don't think it's my fault. I think I still got it. Maybe I should try it with someone else."*)

> ## Having sex regularly helps you to grow old together *gracefully*.

When one of you is suffering from a physical illness, the relationship also suffers. You'll spend too much time, thought, and energy into worrying about the medical bills and the future and when this happens, tenderness and affection takes a backseat. The fact is, when you're too preoccupied with your own pain, you don't have much care left in you to share with your partner. Moreover, couples with poor levels of health are prone to irritability and thus, making them vulnerable to domestic disputes.

A romp in the sheets is a fun and pleasurable way to burn calories. By turning sexy time into your cardio, you're helping each other stay physically fit. Regular sex reduces the risk of bone diseases (pun not intended), heart disease, and prostate cancer. Keep those hormones flowing to get the benefit of glowing skin and to tame those merciless menopausal symptoms. Sex is also a great immune system booster. Likewise, it enhances your capacity to deal with stress. Improve each other's health and prolong each other's lives so you can make more beautiful memories together.

Chapter 2

How to be Sexy in the Bedroom and How to Maintain a Great Sex Life

When you and your long-time lover have been at it for years, it has the following effects:

- less self-consciousness
- less mystery
- less spontaneity

> ➤ **Successful couples pay attention to pre-sex prepping.**

Your partner has seen it all so you shouldn't have to worry about shaving off your pubes, right? And since you love each other, it shouldn't matter if you skip the shower, right? Wrong! Being married for years and even being madly in love is no excuse for shortchanging your sexual soulmate. You need to perform pre-sex prepping as diligently as you did during the honeymoon phase of your relationship. Wear cologne like you used to. Invest in sexy lingerie like you used to. This will prevent your spouse from forgetting what attracted him/her to you in the first place. Furthermore, prepping your body for sex makes your partner feel special. It makes them feel that you still value what they think and that their desire is still worth earning.

The problem with some couples is that they find it awkward to talk to each other about sex and hygiene. To others, it's easier to just have sex less often than to risk embarrassing, provoking, or hurting their partner in a conversation about stubbles and body odors. So don't wait for your husband/wife to tell you that you need to take care of yourself because they probably won't. It's your job anyway and no one has to tell you to do these things. To put it bluntly: If you want more oral action, shave your nether regions.

That said, pre-sex prepping doesn't have to be a boring chore. In fact, you can even do it together. Start your foreplay in the shower by soaping each other's bodies.

> ➢ **Smart couples know that they have to look, think, feel, and be sexy.**

When you no longer find yourself attractive, this lowers your libido. Low self-esteem cripples your capacity to become open to new sexual adventures. A woman might be afraid of trying a new sex position because she's worried about how big her butt will look like. A man might feel threatened by prolonged foreplay because he might be unable to maintain his erection. In order to be sexy, you need to look, think, and feel the part. Preparing your body for sex shouldn't be done just prior to a lovemaking session. Instead, it should be something that you incorporate in your lifestyle. When you exercise, maintain a balanced diet, and rehydrate you are priming your body for lovemaking. A positive body image will make you more confident in bed. Provide yourself with positive affirmations (ex. "My body is beautiful.", "I am sexy within and without.")

Being physically fit will significantly improve your bedroom performance. Additionally, kegels exercises for women helps in toning the butt, the lower back, and the abdomen so she can effectively use these muscles to position herself during sex. Thus, allowing her to get more G-spot stimulation and more orgasms. Likewise, kegels exercises for men will help him in achieving ejaculatory control. Meanwhile, specific exercises like ball crunches can help improve his thrusting power.

> ➢ **Clever couples understand that familiarity breeds boredom.**

Sure, you've memorized every hair, every mole and explored every nook and cranny of each other's bodies but this is not an excuse to let the mystery jump out the window. Mystery equals to excitement and it's something that we all subconsciously crave. When this element disappears, that's when you start wondering and fantasizing about how it would feel like to have sex with other people. Not everyone will act on these fantasies but unfortunately, there are those who do.

To keep your spouse from straying, change things up in the bedroom. It doesn't have to be a drastic change. It can be as simple as a haircut or a new sex position that you haven't tried before. Readjust your carnal clock. That is, if you're used to making love in at night, rub up against your spouse early in the morning. Turn familiar objects and places into things and areas of mystery. Example: Make pantry staples even yummier by introducing food into foreplay. Surprise your spouse with an erotic buffet by placing fruits, whip cream, chocolate, and other edibles all over your body for him/her to feast on. Your partner will never see the kitchen in quite the same way.

> ➢ **A passive lover is no lover at all.**

So, are you a person or a blow-up doll? When you just lie there like you're bestowing your spouse a grand favor, you make your partner feel as though he/she is not worth your effort. This, in turn, kills their motivation, leading to mediocre performance. Furthermore, letting your partner do all the work implants in his/her brain that sex is nothing more than a routine activity. Remember that nothing can kill passion quicker than monotony. Motivate your partner by taking the lead from time to time. Sex should be a complete tactile, visual, and auditory experience. Even when your lover is on top, motivate him/her by sexy sounds and facial expressions. A woman can touch herself while her husband is making love to her. Likewise, a man can whisper words of affection (or talk dirty) while his wife is making love to him. Even when your partner is doing all the thrusting, do your part by stroking, kissing, and licking his/her erogenous spots. Moreover, eye contact deepens the intimacy of the act so even when you're all tied up, you can still participate by expressing your love (and lust) through your eyes.

> **Wise couples don't just do it. They talk about it.**

If there's anything that's more intimate than having sex, it's talking about sex. You become sexier to your partner if you can listen to his/her sexual suggestions with an open mind. Stay in tune with each other's erotic desires by openly discussing your fantasies and fetishes. Make a bucket list of the sex positions that you'd like to try, places that you'd like to have sex in, games and toys that you'd like to introduce in the boudoir, etc. Be sure to make this a fair give and take activity. When your partner feels that you're that one person in the world who can listen and make love to him/her without judgment and inhibitions, that's when you're at your sexiest.

Chapter 3

50 Best Sex Positions for Men and Women

Rear Entry Positions

Men love entering women from behind because this position feels very primal. Rear entry positions are also favorable for women who love a strong feeling of fullness during intercourse.

> ➢ **Traditional Doggie Style**

In this position, the woman gets down on her hands and knees with her legs somewhat apart. After this, the man positions himself on his knees and penetrates her from behind.

> ➢ **Turtle Style**

The woman kneels on the floor and then brings her body downwards. She does this so that her buttocks are lying on the back of her ankles. Next, she leans her body forward as far as it can go. The man then penetrates her from the rear.

> ➢ **Frog Style**

To do this, the woman should assume a squatting position. Then, she needs to lean forward. She should place her hands in front of her and make sure that they're flat on the floor.

This will help her balance herself. Next, the man kneels behind her and enters her ala traditional doggie style.

➢ Basset Hound Style

The woman first positions herself on all fours. Next, she has to lower her body onto the floor, spreading her knees outward while pushing her buttocks up towards her partner. She then lowers herself to her elbows so that her chest is near the floor. Afterwards, the man penetrates her from behind.

➢ Corner Doggie Style

The woman assumes a standing position while placing one of her legs on either side of the bed corner. After this, she leans over toward the bed while supporting herself with her elbows. Next, the man enters her from the rear just as he would during the traditional doggie style.

➢ Rear Admiral Style

The couple starts off by standing while facing the same direction. Then, the man penetrates the woman from behind. After this, she bends over so that her abdomen is parallel to the ground. One of them should spread his/her legs open while the other keeps his/her own together. The couple can decide to take turns.

➢ Fire Hydrant Style

The first thing to do would be to have the woman position herself like she would in the traditional doggie style. Her partner should position himself behind her on his knees. He will then lift one of his legs, bring it forward, and place his foot on the ground to the woman's side. As he does this, he lifts her leg. This way, her thigh will be lying on top of his thigh.

- ➢ **Bulldog Style**

Compared to the classic doggie, the bulldog places the woman on a more submissive role. She gets down on her hands and her knees. Then the man and the woman have to bring their legs together. Afterwards, the man squats down a bit and then penetrates his partner from behind. His feet are situated outside of the woman's legs. Meanwhile, his hands are around her waist.

Deep Entry Positions that'll Make Husbands Go Crazy

Men love the feeling of going in deep into their partner. Apart from the exquisite physical pleasure that makes them want to ejaculate quickly, it provides them with a feeling of power and abandon.

- ➢ **Anvil Style**

In this position, the woman lies on her back. Meanwhile, she should keep her legs wide open. The man then lifts the woman's legs towards her chest. Afterwards, he moves over her, using his arms to support himself. Next, he asks her to rest her lower legs on either side of his head so they're touching his shoulders.

- ➢ **Drill Style**

The couple begins with the traditional missionary position, with the woman on her back and the man on top of her. Then, the woman spreads her legs. The man moves on top of the woman. As he does this, she draws up her legs and uses them to embrace her lover's waist.

➢ Deep Impact Style

Lying on her back, the woman points her legs skyward. Meanwhile, the man is to position himself on his knees facing her. Then, she rests her legs on each of her partner's shoulders. Next, he grabs her by the thighs and performs deep thrusts.

➢ Jockey Style

The couple begins by having the woman lie face down on the mattress. She's supposed to keep her legs together. Meanwhile, her lover straddles her, placing his knees on either side of her waist. This looks like he's riding a horse, hence the name. The jockey is perfect for either anal or vaginal penetration.

➢ Cello Player Style

This is done by having the woman lay on her back and then lift her legs in such a way that they're pointing upward. Meanwhile, the man should kneel upright while penetrating her. Next, the woman rests both her legs on *one* of her lover's shoulders. One of the man's arms is to be wrapped around the woman's lower leg. Meanwhile, his other arm should be wrapped around her thighs.

Dominant Male Positions

The following power positions are for men who like playing the role of the dom in the bedroom. These positions require the woman to be physically vulnerable and at his mercy, so to speak. He also gets total control of the pacing and the power of his thrusts. These are also perfect for women who like playing the role of the sub.

➢ Viennese Oyster Style

The woman lies down on her back and spreads her legs wide open. Grabbing her legs, she pulls them in towards herself until her knees are very close to the bed. Then, to make sure that her legs stay in place, she puts her arms at the back of her knees. The man then penetrates her.

➢ Down Stroke Style

The woman should be lying on the edge of the bed. She needs to raise her legs in the air so that they're pointing upward. Meanwhile, the man is to stand in front of the woman. He grabs the woman's legs and then pulls her body up towards his so he can enter her. Each time he thrusts downwards, he raises her body to meet his.

➢ Bridge Style

The woman should be on all fours. But here's the catch: Her back should be towards the ground and her body should be facing the ceiling. Facing his partner, the man kneels and positions himself between her legs. With his hands grabbing her thighs, he enters her while pulling her body close to his.

➢ Suspended 69

This is actually an exotic oral sex position that requires a great deal of power and flexibility. Be warned that this is a potentially dangerous position so it's not for everyone.

The man first lies down on his back. His feet, however, should be draped on the side of the bed, not so much as dangling, but with his feet played firmly on the floor. Next, his partner is to climb on top of him to position herself in a traditional 69. Keeping her legs together, she hugs her lover's head with them.

After a while, the man should try to sit up. Meanwhile, the woman is to make sure that her legs are still holding the back of her lover's neck. The next and the most crucial step would be to gauge whether it's still comfortable to perform oral sex on each other while maintaining this pose. Then, with the woman's arms embracing the man's waist, he gradually assumes a standing position.

Intimate Positions that Wives Love

Women particularly love sex positions that provide them not just with physical pleasure but also with a feeling of closeness with their partner.

➢ Spooning Style

The couple lies down on their sides while facing the same way. The man should be behind the woman. Then, he penetrates her from behind. The woman moves her top leg forward a bit to help the man enter her as he leans over. He then wraps her in his arms.

➢ Sporking Style

The couple starts by lying on their right side, with the man behind the woman. The woman then leans forward and takes her legs towards her upper torso.

➢ Side Entry Missionary Style

The woman needs to lie on her side while keeping her legs together and bending them a little. She may turn her body to face her partner who will have to be on top of her. He is to enter the woman from behind while he's positioned on his knees. So basically, it's like he's doing the missionary while his woman is in a side-lying position.

➤ Sofa Style

In this position, the man sits on the sofa with his feet flat on the floor. Facing him, the woman then squats on her partner and utilizes her legs to help her move up and down.

➤ Pearly Gates Style

Facing upward, the couple lies together. The man should bend his knees a little and make sure that his feet are planted on the mattress. The woman then lies on top of the man while still facing upward. So it's kind of like an upward version of spooning.

➤ Lotus Style

The man should be seated cross-legged, yoga style. Then, facing her partner, the woman lowers herself onto him. The man and the woman then wrap their arms around each other's bodies.

Positions to Give Women Multiple Orgasms

➤ Butterfly Style

While laying on her back, the woman's hips should be situated near the edge of the bed. The man stands at the foot of the bed and raises her hips, allowing her thighs to rest on his chest. The woman's lower legs should be resting on each of his shoulders.

> ### Criss Cross Style

Lying on her back, the woman raises her legs until they are pointing to the ceiling. Standing up straight, the man enters her. Making sure that the woman's legs are still straight, he crosses them at the ankles thus, creating a super tight fit.

> ### Fast Love Style

In this position, the man lies down with his knees slightly bent and his feet flat on the floor. The woman then straddles him while's she's on her feet. This is a nice quickie position for women who feel a sudden urge.

> ### Missionary Style

The woman lies on her back while keeping her legs open. Her partner positions himself on top of her in such a way that his legs are situated between hers. For support, the man may rest his elbows on either side of his partner.

Positions for Maximum G-spot Stimulation

> ### Bent Spoon Style

The man lies on his back and the woman lies on top of him, also on her back. This way, they're both looking up the ceiling. The man penetrates the woman. Meanwhile, she extends her arms outward. The man needs to keep his legs open. Then, the woman draws her knees up towards her upper body and allows her feet to rest on top of her lover's knees.

> ### Italian Hanger Style

The couples needs to first have sex in the classic missionary position. Then, somewhere during the middle, the man gets on his knees, bringing them close to his partner's body. As a result her legs will be spread wider apart. Then, he places his hands beneath her buttocks and raises her hips. He then proceeds with his thrusts.

Positions for Maximum Clitoral Stimulation

➤ Coital Alignment Technique

The woman lies on her back with her partner on top of her. How is this different from the missionary? He has to move his body forward over the woman's as opposed to thrusting in and out of her. This changes the angle of penetration so that his penis is able to stimulate her lower vaginal wall. This way, his pubic bone is in direct contact with her clitoris.

➤ Thigh Tide Style

Lying on his back, the man tries to keep his legs straight while spreading them to some degree. Then, he lifts one knee in such a way that his foot is planted firmly on the mattress. The woman straddles his raised knee and lowers herself onto her lover's penis with her back against him. Then, she performs up and down movements, which will allow her to rub her clitoris against her partner's thighs.

➤ Sandwich Style

The man penetrates the woman ala missionary style while's she's lying on her back with her legs spread open and pulled back towards her chest. He then places one hand under each of her knees to adjust the angle of penetration.

Woman-on-Top Positions for Fierce Females

Women enjoy these positions because it provides them with a sense of empowerment and allows them to control the pace of lovemaking thus, enabling them to achieve orgasms. Men also love woman-on-top positions because it enables them to relax and just open themselves up for pleasure. Additionally, it provides them with a sensational view of their partner's body.

➢ **Cowgirl Style**

The man lies down on his back while the woman assumes a kneeling position as she straddles him. Her legs are supposed to be situated on either side of her lover's waist. She then proceeds to bouncing up and down or grinding on top of him. By moving her body backward or forward, she is able to regulate the angle of penetration.

➢ **Reverse Cowgirl Style**

This is pretty much the same as the cowgirl style. The main difference is that the woman has her back to her partner as she straddles him and bounces or grinds on top of him.

➢ **Asian Cowgirl Style**

This is another variation of the cowgirl sex position. The major difference is that the woman squats with her feet on either side of her lover's body instead of being on her knees. Her feet will therefore be carrying her weight. Her hands may rest on her partner's chest or on either side of him.

➢ **Bucking Bronco Style**

While the man lies on his back, the woman faces him and then gets on top of him. She then guides his penis inside her. After he has penetrated her, she leans backwards while placing her arms behind her. After this, she places her feet on either side of her partner's head.

➢ Rodeo Style

This sex position is a variation of the reverse cowgirl. Facing towards her partner's feet, the woman straddles him while on her knees. The man's job here is to thrust really hard and fast, almost as if he's attempting to buck his partner off him. Meanwhile, she holds on tight and rides the rodeo!

➢ Amazon Style

In this dominant woman-on-top position, the woman asks her partner to lie on his back and tells him to draw his legs up and bend his knees. As he pulls his legs towards his upper torso, she squats down on him and carefully pulls his penis backwards to guide him inside her.

➢ Crab Style

While lying on his back, the man should keep his legs together. The woman then straddles him, placing her legs on either side of his body. After this, she leans backward with her hands and arms extended behind her. She makes love to him by moving her body up and down while using her arms for support. She may also choose to perform rotating maneuvers with her hips.

➢ Missionary Style with Woman on Top

This is different from the traditional missionary style because the woman will be taking the top position. The woman should first ask her partner to lie down with his legs straight. Then, she straddles him while on her knees. Next, she leans her body forward and rests her elbows on the bed.

Man-on-Top Positions for Women who Love Dominant Men

Women love having sex with men who are confident and know what they're doing in bed. By taking control, he is allowing her to just relax and focus on receiving pleasure.

> ➢ **Cowboy Style**

While on her back, the woman makes sure that she keeps her legs together as her partner straddles her. The man's legs are situated on either side of her body. Meanwhile his bum is resting right on top of his partner's legs.

> ➢ **Deckchair Style**

The couples start off in the missionary position. Then, the man gets into his knees while inserting his arms under the each of the woman's knees. His hands are placed on the bed for support. Meanwhile, the woman remains positioned on her back while raising her legs into the air. By assuming this position, they get to stimulate areas that don't get much attention when having sex in the traditional missionary position.

> ➢ **Launch Pad Style**

The woman lies on her back. Meanwhile, the man is on his knees facing her. He enters her and as he does this, she raises her legs skyward, drawing her knees towards her upper body. Then, she allows her feet to rest on her partner's chest.

➤ **Victory Style**

The man is on top while the woman lies on her back and spreads her legs open, holding it up in a V shape. The man then performs thrusting movements while on his knees.

➤ **Exposed Eagle Style**

It's best to begin this position with the classic cowgirl. Once there, the woman leans backward until her back is on top of her lover's knees and his thighs. Then, the man lifts the upper part of his body so that he's seated upright.

Quickie Positions

Nothing turns on a man or a woman more than knowing that his/her sex soulmate wants to have sex with him/her anytime, anywhere. As such, you must have an arsenal of quickie sex positions up your sleeve.

➤ **Bodyguard Style**

Couples start off by standing upright and facing the same way. The man should be positioned behind the woman. Then, with the back part of her body pressed against his front, he penetrates her from behind.

➤ **Bendover Style**

The couple first performs the bodyguard sex position. After he's inside her, she leans her body forward with her arms extended. She lowers her body until her hands are resting on the ground. Then, the man starts thrusting in and out of her.

➤ **Burning Man Style**

This sex position is best done on a countertop. The woman bends over so that her tummy is resting over the countertop. Meanwhile, her feet should be planted firmly on the floor. This will help keep her in place because this position is designed for hard and fast thrusting, hence the name. Her partner then proceeds to entering her from the rear. Couples can use this whether they want to make love vaginally or anally.

➢ Dancer Style

The couple stands facing each other. Then, the woman raises one of her legs and envelops her man's body with it. Next, the man penetrates her and begins thrusting. To make sure that his partner stays in place, the man may wrap his arms around her while supporting her raised leg with his hand.

➢ Pump Style

If you want to have sex by a wall, perform this position by having the woman assume a sitting position in the air. The woman's legs should be bent a little. The man stands beside her and penetrates her from the rear. He then proceeds to thrusting in and out while grabbing onto her waist. To keep herself steady, she may extend her arms and press them against the wall.

50 Sex Positions for Men

The Ultimate Guide to the Best Techniques to Turn Her On

Introduction

I want to thank you and congratulate you for downloading the book, *"50 Sex Positions for Men: The Ultimate Guide to the Best Positions to Turn Her On"*.

This book contains proven steps and strategies on how to give her the biggest orgasms with the most exciting sex positions while still giving yourself a fun time.

The sex positions discussed in this book are selected based on the level of pleasure they can give your woman. Nevertheless, they are still guaranteed to give you intense pleasure to make them your favorite positions as well. Try them out and find what works best for the both of you.

Thanks again for downloading this book. I hope you enjoy it!

How to Get Her in the Mood for Sex

Sex ideally starts with a little teasing, an extended foreplay, a mind-blowing oral stimulation, and ends with an intense exchange of thrusts and grinding. Most men focus on the latter stages and yes, they can make their women orgasm even by proceeding to the action right away. However, if you want to give her the best experience by introducing a big orgasm, you need to start right: by turning her on getting her in the mood.

These nine tips should make that task a breeze.

1. Set the ambience.

Women are easily distracted, so trying to touch her clit as she watches her favorite daytime drama may not work quite well. Instead, be romantic and make the ambience scream of sex. Dim the light, turn down the music, spray her favorite scent, and if available, put her sex toys on the bed.

2. Extend the foreplay.

Foreplay is like a gentle massage: the longer you do it, the more relaxed she gets. In this case, the longer you do it, the hornier she gets. A lot of kissing, cuddling, groping, caressing, and rubbing should do the work.

3. Be gentle with your touching.

Most women like it soft, at the beginning at least. They like to feel that they are being loved and cared for. They like to be reassured that they are safe and not only to be used for sex.

4. Get hot with words.

Dirty talking works well most of the time, especially when it reveals a persona that she is not used to seeing from you. She will take that as a naughty surprise.

5. Be mentally stimulated together.

Watch porn or sex instructional video together. Read an adult article together. Read aloud a naughty erotic book or short story.

6. Play along her fantasies.

Ask what she wants and how she fantasizes you. Even better, ask what her fantasies about you are and bring them to life.

7. Dance for her.

Do you know why Channing Tatum's Magic Mike was a big hit even when it only essentially had women as viewers? It is because women love dancing men while slowly stripping to a horny song.

No abs? Her emotional connection with you will make her ignore that.

8. Play with your body in front of her.

Seriously, do it. You do not have to masturbate in front of her (although it should be done one time or another). Just change clothes, change you underwear in front of her, and take a bath without closing the door.

9. Kiss her.

Nothing turns her on the most but a hot, passionate kiss (preferably with tongue).

9 Cunnilingus Sex Positions to Pamper Her

It turns your woman on to know that you are ready to focus on her pleasure before your very own. How else would you give her the moment but with a long steaming session of cunnilingus?

Cunnilingus means orally stimulating your woman on her vulva, clitoris, and vagina. Your lips and tongue definitely have to work overtime here, but you need a good set of sucking, licking, and tongue-acrobatic skills to master what she considers as the real oral therapy. The positions in this chapter are meant to give her the best orgasms using cunnilingus and the best ways for you to have access to her most precious parts.

1. Her-68 Sex Position

You will be essentially performing the 69 Position, but only you will be facing her pearl to perform the oral stimulation.

Start by lying on your back and letting her lie on top of you but with her vagina on your face. She lies facing upwards while her feet rest on the bed to keep her legs open (which is hard when she is having too much fun). Your only problem in this position is your penis trying to make a hole on her back.

2. Butler Sex Position

This is originally conceived for analingus or oral stimulation of the anus, so it may not be your favorite position. However, with a tongue long and flexible enough to stimulate her from the bottom part of her vagina, this can be a memorable position.

It starts with her standing on the floor with legs slightly spread apart. She should be leaning forward a little to give you better access. You then have to kneel or sit cross-legged behind her and between her legs to start the oral massage.

3. Forbidden Fruit Sex Position

This is the Butler performed while lying down.

She has to lie on her stomach with a pillow under her hips to raise her vagina a bit. You will then kneel between her legs to start pleasuring her. To take the pleasure a notch higher, ask her to raise her hips a little higher to allow your hand to go under. Your hand can play with her clitoris while your tongue dances on her flaps.

4. Drive-Thru Sex Position

This is one of the highest-rated cunnilingus positions because your mouth gets full access on her vagina while she stands patiently to fight the urge to curl in extreme pleasure.

Like in the Butler, she stands with legs slightly open and upper body leaning a bit forward. You, however, will not be kneeling behind her but should go under her while facing her vagina. This will make her appear like squatting on your face. Hold on to her legs to maintain your balance.

5. Eve's Ecstasy Sex Position

This is a great way to give her pleasure and control her movements at the same time.

Lie down across the bed but with your head on the edge. She then straddles on your face to press her vagina onto your mouth. This can be a little uncomfortable to you at first because of the tightness, so she should find her balance to not press hard on your face.

The set-up can be you playing your tongue and lips while she decides how to move her vagina over your mouth.

6. Riding the North Face Sex Position

This is the Cowgirl performed over your face instead of your groin.

Lie on your back but do not forget to use a pillow high enough to give your head a raise. She then straddles your face to keep that tongue and lips near her meat curtains. Asking her to lean backwards a bit will open up her vagina in front of you more.

What makes this position exciting for both of you is her control on her movements and your access to her vagina while also allowing you to play with your penis.

7. Spread Eagle Sex Position

If comfort and pleasure is what your woman is after, this will surely go on top of the list.

She lies on her back, spreads her legs and bends her knees but keeps both feet planted on the bed. You will then take your position between her legs, preferably while lying on your stomach and feet bent upwards. The access her vagina gives you allows your tongue to explore her more, even the insides down to how deep she prefers it.

8. Her-Suplex Sex Position

The level of intensity received by a woman in this position hits the ceiling because of the restriction that makes the stimulation more ticklish.

You first sit on the couch like you would in any normal day. She then lies on the floor perpendicular to you but with her legs raised astride. By this time, you only have to bend forward to reach her vagina. This allows for great clitoral stimulation.

Be sure to place a pillow under her upper back to avoid hurting her shoulders.

9. Under the Sink Sex Position

Imagine yourself fixing the plumbing under the sink, but this time, it will be her hole you are going to look up to.

Lie across the bed with your head protruding down to your shoulders. She then squats on your face to give you access to her vagina. Just small changes in her movements can already give her different clitoral and vaginal stimulations because your mouth practically stays in place while she controls everything.

8 Standing Sex Positions for Intense Thrusting

Standing sex positions are some of the most underrated positions because many couples find them tiring. However, those who have tried a lot of variations will tell you that they are some of the most pleasurable to both men and women. You get to hit her G-spot from behind and stimulate her clitoris from the front while she gets to allow you fast and hard thrusting to make you feel like a real man in control.

These positions will certainly turn her on and keep your blood pumping to your head at the same time.

10. Dancer Sex Position

If you can imagine a common final pose among ballroom dancers where the woman raises one leg to the man's hips, then you have seen what to do. In addition to the intimacy of the eye to eye contact and never-ending kissing, she also gets to moan in pleasure with the intense stimulation of her stretched vaginal walls and clitoris.

Stand facing each other and have her wrap her arms around your neck. Lift her one leg to your waist to open her vagina for penetration. You can thrust fast without sacrificing the intimacy.

11. Ballerina Sex Position

This is a more difficult variation of the Dancer because it requires her great leg flexibility. Like in the last position, stand facing each other while wrapping your arms around each other for support. Instead of raising her one leg to your waist level, it needs to be stretched all the way to your shoulder like what a ballerina would do in a one-foot pirouette.

The way her vagina is stretched will give her new pleasure while you enjoy the tightness.

12. Burning Man Sex Position

This is the Doggy Style done while she leans on a table or counter and you stand behind her. As the term implies, it can get both of you on fire because it allows rapid successions of deep thrusts. You get to stimulate your prostrate from hitting her butt repeatedly and she gets to stimulate her G-spot without having to move at all.

13. Pump Sex Position

You will feel a different kind of orgasm with this position as you penetrate your woman from a very unusual angle.

She straddles a chair while standing up straight. You then crouch on her back, squatting at the end of the chair to reach your target. You have to thrust back and forth while holding her hips to maintain your balance. Moving can be tiring to your legs, but the new pleasure for you and the G-spot stimulation for her are enough rewards.

14. Washing Machine Sex Position

It is as straightforward as it gets—you perform it with the help of a washing machine. This is an extremely exciting and pleasurable position because first, both of you get to enjoy the appliance's vibration; and second, you get to have sex in a different part of the house.

She leans down on the spinning washing machine as she stands in front of it. Stand behind her and start pumping to the tune of the spin.

15. Booster Seat Sex Position

This position can be tiring for you, but may couples who have tried it say that it is a perfect combination of thrill, pleasure, and test of trust.

You stand facing forward on the side of the bed or sofa. Your woman then stands on the edge of the bed or sofa to slowly sit down as you catch her by the waist. You do the necessary adjustments to have a perfect rear entry.

Expect her orgasm to be intense because of the added thrill. The feeling of falling down while receiving pleasure from the bottom is a very special treat.

16. Piston Sex Position

This is designed to give both of you big orgasms because of the fast thrusting it allows. A big bonus for her would be an intense clitoral stimulation.

Stand beside the bed or sofa while facing away and have her straddle you while resting her feet on the edge. Carry some of her weight through her butt to give you extra mobility when thrusting. Pump as fast as you can until both of you can no longer hold it.

17. Stand and Carry Sex Position

Some people say that it is not really a pleasurable position because of the almost total immobility. However, restriction comes with pleasure, especially when your mind forces your body to do everything just to reach orgasm.

From a standing position, carry her completely as she straddles you and wraps her arms around your neck. All the movements can only come down from your waist since you have to concentrate on her weight, but at least you get to turn her on with torrid kissing and lip sucking.

13 Woman-on-Top Positions for Multiple Stimulations

Some of the best orgasms are achieved when women have total control over their movements and angle of penetration. This exactly is the most attractive perk of Woman-on-Top Positions, which is why they love doing them even if they practically have to do everything as their men relax at the bottom. As your woman experiences big orgasms, you also get to relax while enjoying the pleasure as you work less.

Many of the positions in this chapter also add a lot of manual stimulations on the bag. Her position on top usually opens a convenient access to her clitoris and flaps. You love that, do you?

18. Amazon Sex Position

Don't you find it exciting to do a common woman position sometimes? This position does not give deep penetration but it stimulates her vaginal wall a lot. It also gives you intense orgasm as your penis is stimulated while bent backwards.

Lie on your back, raise your hips, and bend your legs until your penis, balls, and butthole are all open to her. This position allows her to squat on top of your penis and do the motion that she prefers. Ask her to move gently as fast movements can hurt your penis.

19. Bucking Bronco Sex Position

This is extremely pleasurable to her because she gets to stimulate her back vaginal wall. At the same time, you get to ejaculate while your penis is bent backwards. Don't even start with how accessible her clitoris is to your hands.

Lie flat on your back and let her straddle you like in a classic Cowgirl Position. Instead of leaning forward though, ask her to bend backwards a bit while your penis is inside her to achieve the desired angle. She should thrust up and down while her arms support her from the back.

20. Corner Cowgirl Sex Position

This is the Cowgirl Position but done while you lie diagonally on the corner of the bed. Half of your legs should be jotting out of the bed.

While she rides on top of you and does her own stimulation exploration, you get to enjoy at the bottom while rubbing her clitoris in front of you. What makes it intense for you though is that you have to keep your legs straight while she grinds. You have to control your leg muscles while containing the pleasure.

21. Crab Sex Position

This is a variation of the Bucking Bronco with slight differences. She has to place her feet forward so that she straddles you from the shoulders while you have to keep your legs close. This still gives her direct control over the angles she wants to be stimulated but you will have a tighter feel in your balls and penis as your legs put pressure on them.

22. Fast Fuck Sex Position

The name alone is enough to turn her on, especially when you whisper in her ear that you want to try it. It is called this way because it allows her to grind, gyrate, and thrust in fast successions while allowing your penis to go deep.

As usual, you lie on your back and she straddles you to accommodate penetration. She can squat or completely kneel, but she has to lean forward so that her weight does not go down to her waist. She can grab your shoulders or prop her arms while you hold her legs as she moves. The movements should come from her waist alone so she can hit the fast fuck meter.

23. Jugghead Sex Position

This has a tinge of BDSM (Bondage, Dominance, Submission, Sadomasochism) because she has to pin your hands up while she moves on top of you. It does not stop there though.

You have to lie down on the floor perpendicular to the bed or sofa because you need to lift your lower body and rest your legs on the edge. She then straddles you while pinning you down. The angle of your raised penis gives her a different stimulation while this position also gives you a different feeling.

24. Lunge Sex Position

Lunging stretches her vagina on the side, which makes stimulation different and more exciting.

Lie on your back and have her stand between your legs. To get into the lunge position, she has to slowly lower her body like squatting, stretch one leg backwards, and place the other leg on your side. As she lunges on top of your penis, have her rock back and forth while you play with her breasts.

25. Man Missionary Sex Position

This is the common Missionary Position but with your woman straddling you on top and your legs bent upwards while keeping them close. She has to completely lean forward once penetration is successful so that her waist can move to any direction as fast as she wants to. Bending your legs, on the other hand, gives you mobility from the bottom to help with the thrusting. Keeping them close also gives your balls and penis a pleasurable pressure.

26. Rodeo Sex Position

This is essentially a Reverse Cowgirl Position where the woman straddles you while facing your feet. However, instead of kneeling and relaxing her butt and legs on you, she has to kneel upright so that her movement is limited to up-and-down thrusting. This resembles a bull trying to knock down a rider.

This can give incredible G-spot stimulation for her and very controlled grip around your penis.

27. Sliding Lady Sex Position

This is the variation of the Coital Alignment Technique (CAT) where your public bone and shaft rub with her clitoris by positioning on top of her a little higher. The difference is that it has to be her to be on top of you.

She straddles you while you lie down but instead of just inserting your penis inside of her, she has to adjust so that the head of your penis rubs against the inner side of her clitoris. She has to slide on top of you instead of thrust up and down.

28. Thigh Tide Sex Position

Another explosive orgasm awaits her with this one as she gets to have intense vaginal penetration while rubbing her clitoris against your thigh. She basically needs to hump your thigh while keeping your penis insider her.

Lie down but keep your legs spread apart. One leg should be bent upwards where she will slide down until penetration is successful. She has to hump as tight as possible to your thigh to enjoy clitoral rub.

29. See-Saw Sex Position

Like in this famous playground ride, her movements on top of you are restricted from side to side.

Start by lying on your back and having her straddle you. Her feet should be a little forward and not kneeling. You have to raise your upper body then to take a sitting position. She grabs your shoulder so as not to lose her balance and in this position, her waist can slide side to side like a see-saw while your penis is stimulated from within. She will be leaning a little backwards, so that gives you an opening to suck and lick her breasts.

30. Side Rider Sex Position

The movements are limited in this position, but she surely won't mind when she feels the pleasure of your penis stimulating the side of her vagina and her G-spot from a different angle.

While you lie down, she slowly sits on top of you and inserts your penis inside her but with both of her feet on your side. The pressure of the stimulation will then go to the side of her vagina and your penis, giving both of you a new experience.

7 Lap Sex Positions That Give Her Control

These positions are performed while your woman is on your lap. It means that she will still have a lot of control over her movements, which is great because she can stimulate herself to her liking until she explodes while still giving you intense pampering. Isn't it exciting to leave majority of the pleasuring decisions to her?

31. Lap Dance Sex Position

Come on, you know this position would be on this list. It is easy, relaxing, but most important of all, pleasurable.

You only have to sit on a couch relaxingly with your legs slightly open. She then sits on your lap as she slides your penis inside her. The position gives her enough freedom to do whatever she wants: grind, gyrate, pump, form figures and shapes, and rock. You can stimulate her clitoris as she wishes.

32. After-Dinner Sex Position

This is a variation of the Lap Dance that is ideally performed after dinner. Instead of sitting on a sofa, you will be sitting on a chair or rather remain on the chair after dinner. She sits on your lap but instead of moving as she likes to, she should only sit still while resting her arms and hands on the table. You have to do the thrusting from the bottom, as hard as you want to.

33. Jellyfish Sex Position

The angle of penetration is something to moan about because of the added pressure your penis gives her clitoris and upper vaginal wall.

It starts with you squatting with your butt resting on your legs. She then straddles you and rests her feet as forward as possible. Wrap your arms around each other for support and start rocking back and forth.

34. Bouncing Spoon Sex Position

It does not look like a spoon, but it is as pleasurable.

Sit upright with your back against the wall or the bed's board. Your legs have to be closed and stretched. She will then stand on either side facing forward before kneeling slowly to allow your penis to slide inside her. She has to lean backwards to rest on your chest and just bounce like a ball on top of your lap as you thrust in and out.

35. Lotus Sex Position

The intimacy of this position is great for her clitoral stimulation. When matched with passionate kissing as you come in and out of her, she has no other way to go but up and feel the heavens.

Sit on the lotus position (cross-legged sitting) and have her straddle you with both legs crossed around you as well. She can rock back and forth and pump up and down until both of you hit climax.

36. Lotus-Kneeling Sex Position

This is basically the same with the lotus position but only she will be sitting in the position. You have to kneel instead of sit cross-legged to give her a more upwards penetration.

37. Side Saddle Sex Position

Your penis bent a bit backwards will give both of you incredible pressure.

Lie on the edge of the bed but with your feet hanging or resting completely on the floor. Spread your legs and have her sit between them as she slides your penis inside her. You have no control over the movements, so it is up to her to move the way she wants to.

7 Face-to-Face Sex Positions to Increase Intimacy

Many positions in the other chapters are essentially performed face to face as well. However, these seven positions can be considered the most intense and intimate as they give both of you more access and mobility.

38. Bended Knee Sex Position

This is a variation of the Dancer Position from chapter 3 where one of your woman's legs is raised to your hips. In this position, however, both of you will be kneeling on one leg while her other leg is lifted on top of your raised leg. Your waists will be free to move while kissing each other passionately.

39. Book Ends Sex Position

This is the Missionary Position done while both of you are kneeling. Both of your legs should be slightly spread apart to make thrusting easier. What makes this incredibly pleasurable, especially for her, is that your penis is giving her clitoris pressure from this angle, especially when you are taller than she is.

40. Deck Chair Sex Position

This position allows deep and powerful thrusting.

Have her lie on her back with legs raised up to her hips. You then kneel between her open legs lean forward to support your body with your arms. Her legs have to be kept raised and bent. While thrusting, you can suck and lick her breasts or kiss passionately.

41. Delight Sex Position

This is another great position for G-spot stimulation and a lot of playing with her breasts and lips. Ask her to sit on the edge of the bed with legs spread apart like she is offering her womanhood to you. Kneel between her legs and start penetrating her from this position.

42. Drill Sex Position

This is like the Deck Chair done deeper and closer. Like in the latter, she has to lie down and raise her open legs. Once you are kneeling between her legs, lean complete forward so that your chest is now touching her breasts. She then wraps her legs around your torso to help you thrust deeper as she wants to. You can imagine a lot of kissing going on here.

43. Folded Deck Chair Sex Position

This is another variation of the Deck Chair but instead of her legs raised and bent, she has to completely bend on the waist and keep her legs straight. You have to kneel in front of her and lean forward with your arms supporting your weight. To keep her legs straight, rest them on your shoulders.

44. Viennese Oyster Sex Position

This is the Folded Deck Chair but more extreme. It requires higher flexibility to your partner because her legs have to bend all the way to her head, stretching her vagina and clitoris to the best way possible. Rather than kneeling, you can be too leaning forward, more like lying on her, because of her position. It makes penetration deeper and her clitoris easier to stimulate.

6 Rear-Entry Sex Positions for a Different Thrill

Many rear-entry sex positions are extremely pleasing to a woman because the angle at which a man's penis penetrates her. Such positions are mostly for well-endowed men, but you can make her scream in pleasure even if you are just average because they are also ideal for manual clitoral stimulation with a lot of caressing and breast rubbing.

45. Acrobat Sex Position

Contrary to common first impression, this position is actually easy to do and can be your woman's favorite.

Lie down and have her straddle you on a kneeling position while facing away so that you end up facing her back. After penetration, have her lean backwards until she is completely lying on top of you. All you have to do is thrust from the bottom, give her a little gyrating space, and make those hands naughty all over her body. Focus on the clit of course.

46. Bent Spoon Sex Position

Carrying something while lying on your back can never be as pleasurable as this one.

Lie down and have her lie on top of you as well. Ask her to bend her knees upwards so that her vagina is now more open to your penis. Penetrate by bending your legs a little bit as well and spoon her from the bottom. Her arms should be spread apart to give your hands the exclusive rights to her breasts.

47. Frog Leap Sex Position

This can be tiring for her because she basically has to squat until both of you *come*, but many women who have tried it swear that the sensation is, well, sensational.

Have her squat and arch her back for balance and easy penetration. You then kneel behind her, hold her waist for support, and pump until you like. The very unusual angle of penetration can be unexpected pleasurable and new.

48. Pearly Gates Sex Position

This is a similar to the Acrobat, but instead of kneeling as she straddles you, she will be lying on top of you with both legs slightly bent and spread apart. You also have to bent and spread your legs a bit open but still between her for maintain your balance for thrusting. Your hands have nowhere else to go but on top of those boobies.

49. Teaspoons Sex Position

You can call this the Pearly Gates done in kneeling position. Both of you have to kneel on the floor, she facing away from you. Her legs should be spread apart but yours should only be slightly open to make thrusting easy. Ask her to hold your waist or but for support while your hands support her by keeping her vagina pressed and her clitoris rubbed playfully.

50. Turtle Sex Position

This is like the Doggy Style but done at a much lower position. Instead of her going down on all fours, she has to kneel and bend her body down until her knees are already touching her breasts. You have to kneel with legs spread apart to go to her level, but her lowered angle will force your penis to bend a little downward, which will give both of you a different sensation.

5 Ways to Guarantee Her Big Orgasm

Find her G-Spot

The G-spot is an erogenous zone in her vagina that has met both great responses and skepticisms since it was first brought out in the media in the 1980s. The scientific community has yet to prove if it exists, but in a more common term, it is the extension of her clitoris. It means that it is her most pleasurable spot inside the vagina.

So why has it been said that you can hit her G-spot in many of the positions? In a general term (or rather media-hyped term), it refers to you hitting her deeper vaginal walls where it is said to be more pleasurable.

Finding her G-spot is exciting because that is exactly the point of trying out different positions. At first, you can try out positions that you are familiar with and have her rate each position according to pleasure. It can be a little game for both of you, which can last the whole night.

Just do not forget that your penis is not as flexible as your fingers and tongue.

Stimulate her clitoris.

The clitoris is easier to see because it is that little gem on top of her vagina that you can play like a switch to turn her sanity on and off as long as you like. What's really great about it is that you can stimulate it in a lot of ways—using your tongue, your lips, your fingers, your palm, your penis, and basically everything that you can rub against it. It is her most sensitive erogenous zone, so sex positions that stimulate the clitoris as well are guaranteed to giver her the big O.

Penetrate her from different angles, with different pressures.

Aside from being a part of finding her G-spot, penetrating her from different angles also gives her different types of pleasures. That also means having your penis stimulated on different angles (it is tantamount to masturbating in different hand positions).

Sex is like food. Eat the same meal everyday and you will no longer find it exciting and pleasurable sooner or later. However, eating a new recipe everyday can keep that excitement alive for a long time.

Penetrating her from different angle is not limited to your penis. Your tongue and fingers can do the job as better.

Touch her sensitive parts.

Do not focus on the target too much. There are other erogenous zones on her body. Caress her breasts and nipples, neck, waist, shoulders, legs, feet, and perineum or the area that separates her vagina and anus. Keep those hands working while your penis takes the lead role. Multiple stimulations can only lead to one thing: the big O.

Condition her mind into receiving only pleasure.

As explained in the first chapter, mental conditioning is very important because the body only accepts pleasure when the mind is also ready to accept it. Turning her on is the best prelude to sex, but reassurance is also a big part of it. Reassure her that your focus is only her and that her pleasure is your priority. Make her feel safe by giving her your word and taking it gently even when you are about to perform a difficult position.

50 Sex Positions for Women

The Ultimate Guide to the Best Techniques to Turn Your Man On!

information is without contract or any type of guarantee assurance.

The trademarks that are used are without any consent, and the publication of the trademark is without permission or backing by the trademark owner. All trademarks and brands within this book are for clarifying purposes only and are the owned by the owners themselves, not affiliated with this document.

Table of Contents

Introduction

I want to thank you and congratulate you for downloading the book, *"50 Sex Positions for Women: The Ultimate Guide to the Best Techniques to Turn Your Man On"*.

This book contains proven steps and strategies on how to give your man the best sex ever while also giving yourself the best orgasms.

This is the complete guide to pleasing your man but still making sure that you are satisfied to the fullest with the most stimulating sex positions for yourself. Some tips to get him into the mood and achieve explosive orgasms are also discussed in this book.

Thanks again for downloading this book. I hope you enjoy it!

The Secrets of Turning Your Man On

Men are as aural as they are visual. They have playful imagination that can quickly turn them on. However, for their imagination to work, you need to do some prodding by giving a little tease.

These are some tips that are guaranteed to work on your man and get him in the mood for sex.

1. Show subtle hints a few hours before your private time.

Do some sexy flicking of your hands and hair or a quick pouting with lip tonguing with or without eye contact. You can also say a lot of keywords that you know affect him the most. Keywords like "blow," "suck," "hard," and "swallow" are normally used in everyday sentences, but your man might hear them differently.

2. Deliver the good news way too early.

If you want his groin to remember you the whole day, say your plan earlier in the day. Whisper in his ear that you are going to suck and play with his balls when he gets home right after riding the car en route to work. You can also text or call him a few minutes after leaving the house.

3. Give him a strip tease.

Your man must be either fatigued or having an anxiety attack to totally ignore you while doing this. The signal does not get as straightforward as this.

4. Tell your plans.

Tell him what you are planning to do with him exactly. Describe how you are going to take off his clothes, caress his body, play with his most sensitive parts, and make him *come* like he has never done before. His imagination will do the rest for you.

5. Hug him from behind.

For some reason, sneaking up on him while he is doing something just to give him a groping hug creates a different sensation. Maybe men just have this natural tendency to imagine your hands going down on them.

The same effect is observed when you climb on top of him while in bed or on the sofa.

6. Join him while bathing.

Bathing is the only time when you get to unofficially start the sex without really admitting it. You get to see him naked, touch each other's body, and play with each other's genitals without getting rid of your excuse. Of course, both of you know that you want to have sex, but you can deny it. It is sexier this way.

9 Fellatio Sex Positions to Keep Him Rock Hard

No man can resist fellatio. Men love it, especially when their partners are willing swallowers. It may not be your idea of turning your man on, but it does not change the fact that it is one of the most tested ways to drive him crazy and make him love you more.

Fellatio requires trust to work, especially when it includes ejaculation inside the mouth. This is why women who do so tend to receive more intimate treatment from their partners.

There are nine fellatio sex positions in this chapter—the most number of positions in any chapter—simply because the point of this whole book is to pamper your man like a king. Don't worry because the succeeding chapters will be all about pampering your man while experiencing the best orgasms you can have.

1. His 68 Sex Position

The name is one number less than the Inverted 69 Position because it is only meant for your man. While the latter requires both of you to face each other's organs on a top-bottom position, this position requires him to just lie face up on top of you while you give him a head down there. You may get much of his weight, so just ask him to use his limbs for a little propping. You will surely drive him crazy as his penis is stimulated from a downward angle.

2. Atten-hut Sex Position

It is commonly called the Standing Fellatio Position, but it is better called this way to avoid confusion over other standing fellatio variations. Your man only needs to stand while you kneel down and swallow him like a hungry vixen. This is an intensely stimulating position for him because he needs to fight the urge to hump, curl his toes, and tiptoe while enjoying the sensation.

3. Fuck Face Sex Position

The name says it all—he fucks you on the face while kneeling over your chest. While it may sound too brazen for some women, it actually makes your man feel hot and special because of the special treatment-treating him like a porn star to be exact. Allowing him to hump while in your mouth does not work well if you have a shallow gagging reflex, but you can expect him to appreciate your efforts more if you allow him to take some control and let you swallow some juice at the end.

4. Cinema Stroke Sex Position

The name is another giveaway. Imagine you and your man inside a cinema while sitting side by side as you give him head. The increased pleasure here comes from the restriction. As a rule, he should stay seated straight like you do not want to be obvious in public while you blow him hard while also sitting straight. There will be a limited access to his balls and full length, but the oral stimulation from the side of his penis should be enough to make him not notice it.

5. Oral Therapy Sex Position

You definitely want to do this if you are looking forward to giving him a memorable treat for a job well done. Like in a relaxing therapy, he may want to spend the whole day having just this. It is pretty simple. Lay him down on a sofa and kneel in front of his penis. Do what you have to do to make him forget his name. A good sucking and licking should make him curl his toes really tight.

6. Peepshow Sex Position

It is not the type where the man puts his penis inside a hole and the woman sucks him from the other side. Nevertheless, you have to insert your head between his legs as he lies on his side just like you are peeping to see his entire manhood from behind. The level of pleasure of this position hits the roof as having this kind of stimulation from a downward angle is quite unusual. What he will even love is that you have open access to his balls. Think about what you want to do with them now.

7. Plumber Sex Position

This is a little advance like the Fuck Face Position. You will also be lying down at the bottom, but instead of him kneeling to get inside your mouth, he will be down on all fours, making you accept his whole length vertically. You have to keep your face straight up, your mouth fully open, and your neck long to avoid gagging. If you cannot handle it for too long, tell him to stop humping so that you can do the action instead.

8. Game's On Sex Position

This is a classic fellatio position where the man sits while you kneel on the floor between his legs. You get to cover his entire length from this position and can even play with his balls if you ask him to raise his legs. The sensation he receives is priceless because he is already in a very relaxing position. Just tell him to keep his hands away because he might press your head downwards, causing you to choke (and possibly hurt your throat).

9. Southern Exposure Sex Position

Many experts call it the ultimate fellatio experience. Your man lies down with legs stretched and raised to expose his entire southern area, including his butthole. This is the ultimate pleasure giver because you can take him whole at an unusual angle, lick and suck his balls, and lick his perineum (the part between the balls and the anus). The perineum is a very sensitive part (some men say that stimulating it is better than having their penis stimulated). It should also be mentioned that having a man's butthole licked can drive him crazy.

6 69 Sex Positions to Drive Him Mad

When you hear the 69 sex position, you obviously think about the Inverted 69 right away. This is where one is at the bottom and the other is on top while orally stimulating each other. Hence, this chapter focuses on the more unusual but more exciting variations.

Like the fellatio, the positions here are oral-genital in nature. Only this time, both will be receiving pleasures at the same time. Many men definitely prefer fellatio, but most of them are also very much willing to engage in a give-and-take session because that is one part of the excitement. Although your man will surely love the idea, it is likely that you will be getting the biggest advantage here because a man's tongue is more active in a give-and-take position. Most women just cannot handle giving and receiving pleasure at the same time, so do not be surprised if you reach an explosive orgasm way too early than he does.

There are six 69 sex positions discussed here, some of which require a little back power than usual.

10. Sideways 69 Sex Position

This is the easiest variation because you and your man only need to orally stimulate one another while lying down side by side. As you give each other a treat, wrap your arms around each other's hips to have more control over your partner's movements. This is perfect for couples who want to feel equal with one another when it comes to sex.

11. Sitting 69 Sex Position

This is where the difficulty goes a little higher. While your man lies down on the edge of the bed with both feet on the floor, you position yourself to assume the usual Inverted 69 Position. He then slowly rises up to assume a sitting position, which puts you now on an upside-down position. Your movements will be limited, but as said before, pleasure also comes from restriction.

12. Kneeling 69 Sex Position

Like in the Sitting 69 Position, you are required to be carried upside-down while your man kneels on the floor (it is important that he is on a stable surface). Let him kneel first with legs slightly spread open before you take your position (most women say that it is easier to assume the position when they stand first). You will have the advantage of sucking him because of your head's mobility but his tongue can surely compensate for that (plus the fact that you will be orally pleasure in an upside down position).

13. Standing 69 Sex Position

As the name implies, you do the position while your man stands upright. The only difference is that your legs should be rested flatly on his shoulders and wrapped around his neck since you will be lifted from a higher level.

Many couples think that they should start with this position first before assuming the kneeling position, believing that it is the transition when the man already gets tired from standing. However, it is not recommended as doing the transition may be dangerous for you. Your weight may be too much for him to balance you while trying to kneel.

14. Face Off Sex Position

Your man will surely feel more excited about this position as you practically open all your pleasure holes in front of his face. While he sits on the floor with legs stretched and spread open, you stand facing the same direction as his before bending down to reach his penis. You need to be flexible to perform this, but your man can reward you with genital pleasure from the back and more clit rubbing from the front using his hands.

15. Golden Gate Sex Position

This is the most advanced 69 variation because it requires great flexibility from you. While he lies down, you lie down facing upwards on him as well to give him direct access to your vagina. However, in order to put his penis inside your mouth, you have to raise your body and bend your neck backwards until you reach him. You will be assuming an arch position (like the frame of the Golden Gate Bridge) while giving him head.

7 Butterfly Sex Positions to Make Him Ask For More

It is hard to tell where the term butterfly came from, but if there is one thing for sure, these positions are not cute and glittery; they are extremely hot!

What makes these seven positions some of the best positions for you and your men is the access he gets to the other parts of your body. His hands usually have some sort of mobility here to play with your breasts, stomach, arms, and of course, clitoris. Why would your man pass up that opportunity and why would you deprive yourself of multiple stimulations?

16. Butterfly Sex Position

Apparently, this is the most basic of all Butterfly Positions. Do not get it wrong though because the pleasure it gives him is nowhere near basic.

Your man will love it because it is like offering yourself to him. In fact, you open your vagina like a welcome banner. You simply have to lie down on the edge of the bed, place your feet on the floor, and spread open that treasure trove. He simply has to kneel down to penetrate you while his one hand plays with your breasts and the other rubs your clitoris until your orgasmic energy bursts out you.

17. Bridge Sex Position

What makes this acrobatic position very pleasing to his eyes is the unusual position you take. It is a big turn on for men to see their partners look like professional porn stars sometimes, but you also have the benefit of being stimulated from a position you rarely do in your life. How is that for a one-of-a-kind experience?

You have to form a bridge by lifting your whole body using all four limbs. While you do this facing upwards, he kneels in front of you to penetrate. His hands ideally hold your legs for support, but they can catch your butt instead to grope and press them passionately.

18. Cradle Sex Position

Although an easier variation of the Bridge, the pleasure he will feel is more intense because of the deeper penetration. Assuming from the Bridge Position, you simply have to lower your hips and ask him to sit on his legs as well to match the level. It will appear that you are resting on his lap while still propping your body. He can perform short but deep thrusts on you.

19. Arch Sex Position

This is another variation of the Bridge, but instead of your hips being lowered, it will be your head that should be rested on the bed. He will still be penetrating while kneeling upright, but that gives him enough mobility to rim you as fast and hard as he wants to. Because he no longer has to support your weight, his hands can enjoy caressing your breasts and clitoris. Lucky you!

20. Cross Sex Position

The tightness of your vagina matters when increasing stimulation during penetration. This is exactly what he gets in this position.

While he lies on his side, lie down at a perpendicular position to him so that your pattern resembles a cross. Place both of your legs behind his butt so that he can enter you from behind. Make sure that your legs are as tight as possible to increase the sensation both of you feel.

21. Deep Impact Sex Position

It is called this way because your man gets to penetrate you deeply. This makes it a good position for men whose size is average.

Like the basic Butterfly Position, you lie on the edge of the bed and make him kneel in front of you. However, your legs will be resting on his shoulders this time so that your vagina is more open and stretched. He can now penetrate deeper with a tighter feeling to it.

22. Deep Stick Sex Position

This is basically the same as Deep Impact, but your man can penetrate you deeper because his penis will be much closer to your vagina. While Deep Impact is performed while you lie on the edge of the bed, this position is performed entirely on top of the bed. He has to spread his legs very open while kneeling to penetrate you deeply, but having his balls bang your butt adds nothing but sheer pleasure.

7 Cowgirl Sex Positions to Make Him Scream in Pleasure

Your man may not admit it, but he likes acting like the boss in bed. That means having to do nothing while you do everything. Consider it a treat or a bribe to make him do what you want next time. In the meantime, concentrate on him and ride him until he screams in pleasure.

As an instant reward, you get to stimulate your G-spot and clitoris intensely because of the angle his penis is penetrating you.

23. Cowgirl Sex Position

You know this basic one would appear here. Why not? Men dig it when women act dominating and proceed to do almost all the work.

As a treat, your man only needs to lie down as you kneel astride him. You initiate the penetration and up-and-down thrusting, but you can also leave some control to him by allowing him to thrust from the bottom.

24. Asian Cowgirl Sex Position

This is a just another variation of the basic Cowgirl where you squat astride him instead of kneeling. It will be a little tougher on you since you will not be able to move fast, but the sensation you can give him is incredibly improved. You will be able to do slower but deeper thrusting. Some men say that the slow penetration feels like having a blowjob.

25. Amazon Sex Position

This is a tough woman-on-top variation, but it will drive him crazy no less. Your man has to lie down and raise his butt while his legs are bent. You may think that it is awkward for him, but he can only anticipate the best when he takes an unusual position like that.

You have to squat on top of his butt to allow his penis to slide inside you. Your feet should be slight forward so that your and his legs appear interlocked. Pump up and down but slowly to avoid hurting him.

26. Riding Astride Sex Position

This is a big treat for him because he is in a "therapy" position while you get to stimulate your G-spot until you explode. As he lies flat on a sofa, squat on top of him on a perpendicular position, but keep your legs tight to give him friction. Initiate the thrusting up and down until your legs can take it. You will feel that the stimulation is a bit different because you are pleasured from the side.

27. Side Rider Sex Position

This one is similar to the Riding Astride but done in bed. It looks more like Asian Cowgirl where you squat not astride but on his side. Like the last position, you can get extreme pleasure because of the unusual angle you are penetrated in, but he will also be blown away because he needs to do less.

28. Sybian Sex Position

If you are not aware what Sybian is, it is a dildo that vibrates and rotates at the same time, giving the user intense clitoris and G-spot stimulation. Now imagine how explosive this can be not only to you but your man as well.

Neither of you have to rotate or vibrate, but the effect of this position gives you same effect. It is like the Cowgirl but performed on an ottoman that is not large enough to allow your man to plant his feet on the floor and you to sit astride.

29. Reverse Sybian Sex Position

This can be more pleasurable to both of you because you get to be stimulated from a reverse angle while he will feel tighter. It is a big bonus that you can play with his balls with both hands.

It is the Sybian Position but you have to sit facing the opposite direction so that he faces your back. It is also easier for you to pump up and down in this position because you can rest your hands on his open legs or on the edge of the ottoman once you get tired.

7 Exotic Sex Positions to Fulfill His Fantasies

Men like it dirty once in a while, so this is your chance to give your man that experience. The exotic positions in this chapter are also perfect in making all your sexual fantasies alive. You need to be warned though. Some of the positions here are as difficult as a gym routine, so get ready for hardcore action.

30. The Wheelbarrow

Any list of top exotic positions cannot be completed without the Wheelbarrow. You get to enjoy extreme stimulation in your G-spot while he gets to *come* on shallow but deep and tight thrusts.

You will serve as the wheelbarrow while he serves as the carrier. Prop yourself with your arms as he lifts you from the hips while standing between your stretched legs. He will penetrate you while carrying half your weight.

31. The Ex Sex

This is sometimes called the reverse Missionary because the difference is that your man penetrates you while facing the opposite direction. Instead of you performing it face to face, you are essentially going to watch his balls dribble on your clitoris while he looks the other direction.

Why is it explosive? You get to stimulate your G-spot while he stimulates his penis from a different angle.

32. Bumper Cars Sex Position

This one is similar to the Ex Sex, but you will be lying on your chest instead. It will be harder for him to do rear entry while facing the opposite direction, but the tightness and tension coming from his bent penis will only make both of you scream in extreme pleasure.

33. The Pile Driver

Performed on the floor, you lie on your back and raise both feet until they reach the floor beside your head. Your man then sits on top of your raised hips to penetrate you by pointing his penis downwards. Again, the tension coming from his bent penis will give both of you a different but memorable experience.

34. Poles Apart

This is considered as the reverse Spoon Position. He penetrates you while both of you lie side by side, but instead of lying while facing the same side, he will be heading to the opposite side. That means he will be in front of your legs.

This is another excellent way to stimulate your G-spot and give him tightness at the same time.

35. Brute Sex Position

Many men who have tried it say that it is difficult but addictive. You lie on your back and raise your legs upright until your vagina is completely on top. He then sits down on your vagina but while facing away (you face his back). Penetration requires his penis to be bent downwards, but that gives your clitoris an extra rub from this position.

36. Worm Sex Position

This is like Ex Sex, but he will be on the bottom this time while you pump from the top. Both of you will still face opposite directions, but your legs need to be open to a 90-degree angle. You do most of the pumping but he can rock your butt back and forth to control the movements.

7 Face-to-Face Sex Positions For Maximum Intimacy

Although some of the already discussed sex positions give you face-to-face access, nothing beats intimacy but these following positions.

37. Side to Side Sex Position

It is like Missionary but on your side. Having sex while lying side by side as you face each other gives intense stimulation because the penetration is not merely in and out or up and down. Rather, the restriction of your hips leaves you with no choice but to grind a bit while thrusting. Imagine having a partially shaking and vibrating penis inside you.

38. Piston Sex Position

The name implies fast successive thrusting, actually with a little grinding. While he stands near the ends of the bed, you straddle him and rest your feet on the edge. The position gives both of you the mobility to thrust deep and fast.

39. Lotus Sex Position

The body positioning is unusual but intimate. He sits cross-legged and you straddle him on his hips. You wrap around your legs around his hips so that each thrust becomes short but deep. This is a perfect position for kissing too. Sweet but hot!

40. Kneeling Lotus Sex Position

Its only difference from the Lotus is that your man should be kneeling and resting his butt on his legs rather than sitting cross-legged. This can be more comfortable for both of you because his legs are on a more natural position while you have a bigger space to sit on.

41. Slow Dance Sex Position

This is like the Missionary but performed while standing. While standing face to face, you slightly open your legs while he keeps his legs closed. When he already penetrates you, the thrusting movement should be up and down and side to side like you are dancing. This is a position with direct G-spot stimulation.

42. Victory Sex Position

This is another variation of the Missionary Position but instead of just spreading your legs apart to give him room, you raise both legs to form the letter V.

Why is it different? Your vagina will be raise, which means the angle becomes different without bending his penis too much. This gives you clitoral stimulation and him deeper thrusting.

43. Mastery Kneeling Position

Imagine the Cowgirl Position performed while he is sitting on a sofa. This is basically it. What makes it exciting is the limited movement he has. You basically take control over the entire session.

7 Rear Entry Sex Positions to Make Him Feel Hotter

Many couples still think about anal sex when talking about rear entry sex. That is wrong. This is still sex through the vagina but from behind, which brings the sensation on a whole new level. Your vagina is stretched and stimulated from behind while his penis enters from a tighter angle. Just the thought of these positions is already enough to make you feel hot.

44. Rear Entry Sex Position

This is how basic it can get. You lie on your stomach legs spread and he lies on top of you for a rear entry. Aside from the G-spot stimulation and the burning experience you give him, you get additional stimulation from his pubic bones rubbing your butt cheeks.

45. Doggy Style Sex Position

This chapter is not complete without this one. It is easy. You go down on all fours   and he kneels behind you between your legs before he thrusts in and out. He gets to penetrate you while playing all over your body and you get to experience additional stimulations on your back, neck, nipples and your favorite spot, clitoris!

46. Bulldog Sex Position

The "dog" in the name is a giveaway, but it is a little different because instead of him kneeling behind you, he will be squatting with his feet placed outside of your legs. The thrusting motion will not be as fast as the classic Doggy Style, but it will be deeper and harder.

47. Final Furlong Sex Position

This is exciting because you get to have sex while both straddling an ottoman. You straddle facing the same direction and do the entry in this position. By bending a little forward, your clitoris can be rubbed against the ottoman while his balls are also done the same. It is not everyday that you experience this, right?

48. Bodyguard Sex Position

It does not have anything to do with the movie (unlike the Pile Driver, which came from a movie), but it does look like a bodyguard rimming the client from behind. It is basically having sex while standing facing forward. Your hands grabbing his butt and his hands rubbing your clitoris and breasts are big bonuses.

49. Jockey Sex Position

This is basically the classic Rear Entry but as the name implies, he rides on top of you like a jockey on a race. He straddles you and leans forward while thrusting in and out. His forward position adds tension to his penis, which makes it very pleasurable to both of you.

50. Ben Dover Sex Position

This is the Bodyguard that requires you to bend over at your waist until you are already looking upside down and your vagina opened from behind. Flexibility is a requirement here but when achieved, you get to understand what simultaneous clitoral and G-spot stimulation really is.

The Secrets to Better Orgasms

1. Get stimulated at a different angle.

You see a lot of positions mention stimulation from a different and unusual angle. Why does it matter?

A man's erection has a natural angle, which is upright (pointing upwards). This is the same angle that his penis takes when penetrating a woman using common sex positions, such as the Missionary and Spoon. In fact, this is the same angle that almost all men are used to having orgasm through masturbation. In other words, this is an ordinary angle for him to reach orgasm.

Stimulating him from a different angle, such as when his penis is slightly bent downwards or when you stimulate him from the side, is more pleasurable because it is something that does not frequently happen. Hence, the orgasms in these angles are more explosive.

The same is true for women since their vagina is naturally open upwards.

2. Prolong the excitement.

Excitement builds libido. The higher the libido means better orgasm for both of you. This is why foreplay is crucial in a couple's sex life. It stimulates you and your partner not just physically but also mentally and emotionally. You get to play with your fantasies and stimulate your imaginations.

You probably notice that sex is better when you and your partner are so wet already before the penetration begins. It is a sign that your libido is really high and that your brains are already conditioned to travel for orgasm.

There are a lot of ways to prolong excitement, such as prolonging foreplay and starting your teasing game earlier but delaying the actual sex at a later time. Just remember that excitement is not necessarily stimulated physically because the mind is more powerful than the skin.

3. Stimulate your most sensitive parts.

Your most sensitive parts are the clitoris, G-spot, and nipples. His most sensitive parts are head of the penis, frenulum (the skin that folds and loosens up under the head), perineum (the part between his balls and anus), and nipples. Focusing on these spots while having sex will give you intense orgasm.

Many sex positions in this book stimulate your clitoris and G-spot, if not give your partner the chance to manually and orally stimulate them while having penetration. Similarly, many positions give him a tighter grip that stimulates his penis very well. Also, the point of the fellatio positions is to maximize his pleasure points, including the perineum.

4. Prepare your mind.

Putting your mind somewhere else while doing the deed will stop you from reaching orgasm regardless of how intense the sex positions are. Sex is half physical and half mental. Conditioning your mind to appreciate the deed and anticipate great pleasure is basically half of the excitement and lust. Also focusing your mind on the journey towards climax will make everything more memorable and real.

Do not have sex if you cannot put your 100% into it because a series of bad sex just creates mental fatigue that takes out the fun in your sex life.

Marriage and Sex:

Why sex matters to keep romance alive!

Introduction

I want to thank you and congratulate you for downloading the book, *"Marriage and Sex: Why sex matters to keep romance alive!"*

This book contains proven steps and strategies on how to achieve a successful marriage by increasing the quality of your sex life.

The longer you've been married to each other, the more roles you end up taking. With each day, you become more of a mother, father, provider, or homemaker and less of a lover. Some couples feel that as long as they are able to fulfill these other roles, it should be enough to keep their home and marriage intact. Yet, studies reveal that it doesn't make much difference how many kids you've got, how long you've been together, or whether you live in a low-income or a high-income household. The fact is: Lack of sex and intimacy result to unhappy marriages and broken homes.

Sex between married couples is different from sex between non-married couples. Instead of a quick, physical interaction, sex in marriage becomes a deep, meaningful, affirming connection which strengthens the couple's relationship. Sleeping with the same person for years mean that you know exactly where and how he/she wants to be touched. You know what each gesture, each sigh, and each look means. Furthermore, the longer you've lived together under the same roof, the more comfortable you've grown with each other. Sex between married couples is free from inhibitions. Instead, the act itself becomes an expression of total acceptance. Because of this, sex becomes more pleasurable and more satisfying. So why aren't you doing it as often as you should?

A lot of stuff tends to get lost in a typical household: socks, spontaneity, sex...

Through this book, you will learn:

- the importance of sex in marriage
- sex positions that your husband/wife will love
- why couples lose their sex drive and strategies on how to regain it
- secrets for maintaining a great sex life

Thanks again for downloading this book, I hope you enjoy it!

Chapter 1

Why is Sex Important in Marriage?

> ➢ **Sex is unique between you and your spouse.**

Among the many ideal characteristics of marriage is that it enables couples to share sexual intimacy with each other and *only* with each other. The fact that the two of you are married makes sex more valuable because it becomes a pleasurable experience that you can uniquely and exclusively share with your spouse and not with anyone else. Without sex, your husband/wife is literally reduced to the role of a roommate. Thus, the fact that sex is essential to a successful marriage is certainly an understatement.

> ➢ **Sex makes married life a whole lot easier.**

When married couples allow sex life to jump out of the window, this creates a massive strain in the relationship. This may not always be obvious but little by little, the effects manifest themselves through lack of patience, irritability, insecurities, doubt, and subconscious resentment. On the other hand, married couples who have active sex lives tend to be more relaxed. They become happier, more tolerant, and more open-minded. Simply put, sex in marriage helps in smoothing over the trials that married couples inevitably encounter on a daily basis. You'll be surprised to find out how, after solving the sexual issues in your marriage, everything else will eventually fall into place.

➢ Sex is a form of intimate communication.

Sex in marriage involves a deeper level of communication which you can't have with just anyone. Having sex and talking about sex with your spouse makes you vulnerable to him/her and this is a beautiful thing. This validates emotions of trust, honesty, and acceptance. Telling your spouse where and how you would like to be touched brings you to a comfort level which you will never feel with anyone else. Your husband/wife is that one person in the universe who can see, understand, and appreciate you like no other. With that knowledge in mind, each time you have sex, it becomes more than just a physical act but a powerful emotional experience of giving and receiving with no fear of rejection or judgment.

There is a unique energy between husbands and wives that cannot be expressed in any other way than through sex. But the less couples have sex, the less they become in tune with each other. Eventually, both end up feeling as if the other is a stranger. Come to think of it, having a stranger in your bed is unsettling and frightening. When this happens, all those feelings of trust, safety, and security which are all vital ingredients in marriage just vanish.

➢ Sex affirms your spouse's value.

The typical situation in problematic marriages goes like this:

The husband wants to have more sex while the wife doesn't. For the husband, sex is what enables him to feel close to his wife. The wife cannot understand why he needs sex in order to feel close. She doesn't see why he can't achieve a sense of closeness through talking, cuddling, and just spending time with her. Meanwhile, the husband cannot understand why sexual intercourse does not make his wife feel close to him. Then, the wife begins wondering why sex is so important to her husband. She begins wondering whether there's something wrong with her.

The reason for this is because men and women are wired differently. While women associate romance with emotions, men's perception of romance is strongly associated with sexual affirmation. For men, sex is a verification of their vitality. Sex, especially certain forms of sex such as oral sex, affirm his manhood and makes him feel that you love, respect, and honor all of him.

Here's another typical real life scenario:

The wife worries why her husband lacks interest in her. She does her best to be attractive from spending long hours at the gym to walking around the house in lingerie that are too slutty for her tastes. Yet, the most response she gets from him is a reminder to iron his shirt in the morning. She begins to worry why her husband no longer finds her sexy. This realization damages her self-esteem. She starts feeling embarrassed for having to constantly seduce him. She begins to worry that he's seeing someone else or that she's just not as hot as younger women. Soon, she develops resentment towards her husband.

In both cases, the ultimate effect is emotional detachment between the couples.

What men fail to understand is that their sexual advances make their wives feel special. She needs constant reassurance that you love her and that you still find her attractive after all these years. In other words, your sexual advances affirm her value. All in all, whether you're a man or a woman, you like to feel wanted and needed in your marriage.

> ## Sex protects your marriage.

Lack of sex in marriage brings about infidelity which often leads to divorce. Sexual desires are meant to be shared and not repressed. All of us possess an inborn desire to have sex. But when couples are no longer able to obtain romance, intimacy, and pleasure in their marriage, it creates a void within them which makes them vulnerable to sexual temptation. They end up seeking this much-needed sense of joy and satisfaction elsewhere. It may be through extramarital affairs, sexual fantasies about other men/women, masturbation and pornography, etc.

> ## Sex helps you keep in touch with who you are as a couple and as an individual.

If you've been married for several years, this means you've inevitably acquired new roles other than that of a lover. You become a parent, a provider, head of the household, etc. You become too absorbed with being mom or dad that little by little, you forget who you were as a couple. Worse, you forget who you are as an individual. Dinner dates are replaced by family dinners. Sexy time is replaced by playtime with kids. Personal hobbies that you used to be passionate about are replaced by PTA meetings, soccer games, and ballet recitals. Add to that the hours required for housework and the demands of your career and you'll certainly be left with zero time for your spouse, let alone yourself. There are some couples who think this is okay. After all, you're expected to make certain sacrifices for your children. However, once the children are all grown up and have left the house, most couples are surprised to realize that they have nothing in common with each other anymore.

This is why increasing the frequency and the quality of sex in your marriage is so important. Sex with your spouse reminds you what brought you together in the first place. This doesn't just pertain to the physical attraction but also to the emotional and mental connection that made you want to spend the rest of your life with that person. Sex with your husband/wife will remind you that you're more than just a mom/dad but vital sexual beings with needs and desires.

> ➤ **Sex allows you to stay together longer.**

Physical illness can cause a great strain in your married life. That said, sex is one way in which you can be healthy together. Scientific studies show that sex has several positive effects to your overall wellness. Sexual intercourse stimulates your immune system and improves your stress levels. Older married men who have sex regularly are less prone to developing prostate cancer. Likewise, sex regulates hormone levels so women who have sex more frequently suffer less from menopausal symptoms. Sex also lessens the risk for heart disease in both men and women.

Chapter 2

Best Sex Positions for Him

> ➤ **Doggie Style**

Why your husband will love it:

Generally, men love rear-entry positions because they place them in a position of control. This means that he can regulate the thrusts, to slow it down or speed it up depending on what works best for him. The doggie style is a very primal position and such positions make him feel very manly.

Furthermore, this sex position allows deep penetration so this makes him feel like he's giving you all that he's got and likewise, he's taking all that you have. Additionally, your husband gets a great view of your rear.

Why you'll love it too:

This position can provide you with a full sensation that's really intense.

How to do it right:

- First, you'll need to get down on your hands and on your knees.

- Make sure that your legs are spread slightly apart.

- Your husband will then get down on his knees and then enter you from the rear. He may either place his hands on your back or he may grab your waist if he wants to perform harder thrusts. Alternatively, he may hold on to your shoulders. Or if you're in the mood for rough sex, allow him to grab your hair.

- If you want your husband to go deeper into you, meet his thrusts by pushing your backside against him.

- If you want to change angles, you may lower your body onto the ground.

- You may also make use of your free hand to stimulate your clitoris. Or you may take your husband's hand and guide it towards your love button.

- Maintaining this position can be a bit problematic on your part unless you've got great arm strength. Here's a valuable tip: Try performing this position on the floor by the bed. This way, you can remove your weight off your hands and rest the upper part of your body.

> **Cowgirl Position**

Why your husband will love it:

Most husbands wish their wives would do Woman on Top positions more often. Nobody wants a passive partner in bed.

But more than that, one of your husband's primary goals during sex is to please you. Knowing that he is able to satisfy you physically boosts his ego. Additionally, the cowgirl position provides him with a full view of your body. Remember, men are very visual creatures.

Why you'll love it too:

This position can provide you with a sense of empowerment. Being on top will allow you to regulate the pace, depending on what you think works best for you. More importantly, this ensures that his penis hits all your right spots. Thus, your chances of achieving orgasm in this position ranges from huge to inevitable.

Furthermore, if you'd like to tease your husband or prolong his pleasure, this power position can help you do that.

How to do it right:

- Your husband should be lying on his back.

- Afterwards, you'll have to straddle him while you are kneeling. Make sure that your legs are situated on either side of your husband's waist.

- Move yourself up and down. If you want to adjust the angle, do this by simply leaning forward or backward. Doing so will provide more stimulation for your clitoris and your outer vagina.

- You may choose to rest your hands on your hubby's chest. To maintain intimacy during sex, it's best to remain in contact with whatever body part you can get hold of. That's the other advantage of this position. It allows eye contact between you and your partner so lovemaking becomes more intimate.

- Try having sex in this position with the lights on. This way, he can see your curves. Let go of your feelings of self-consciousness. Also, since your husband gets a full view of your face, drive him mad by biting your lip or with sexy facial expressions. You're in the spotlight so put on a show!

> **Reverse Cowgirl Position**

Why your husband will love it:

He'll love it for the simple reason that it gives him an awesome view of your butt.

Why you'll love it too:

You'll love this for the same reasons that you'll love the cowgirl position. The difference is that this'll keep your frontal curves hidden from your hubby's view. This one's a recommended baby step if you're not ready to get past your feelings of self-consciousness.

How to do it right:

- First, ask your hubby to lie on his back.

- Then, assume a kneeling position and with your back to him, straddle your husband. Your knees must be on either side of his body.

- Perform the trusts by moving up and down, slow or fast or alternate.

- If you want to adjust the angle, just lean backward or forward.

- If you want to switch things up a bit, try making slow grinding maneuvers with your hips.

> **Bodyguard Position**

Why your husband will love it:

This is basically just a classic standing position. Men tend to love it because it's perfect for let's-have-sex-here-and-now moments. This is something that you can do when you're standing by the sink in the kitchen or in cramped rooms when you sneak off for an afternooner. Furthermore, by holding on to your waist, he'll be able to perform harder, deeper thrusts. With this position, the mood can easily change from romantic to rough.

Why you'll love it too:

Even though it's a position for quickies, the Bodyguard isn't necessarily devoid of intimacy. With your back pressed against his front, your husband can nibble on your ear, kiss your neck, or whisper sweet, sexy words while having sex.

How to do it right:

- Begin with the both of you standing upright. You should both be facing the same direction.

- Then, allow your hubby to enter you from behind.

- Meet his thrusts by pushing your body back onto his.

> ➤ **Bendover Position**

Why your husband will love it:

This is another rear-entry standing position that's perfect for quickies. Much like the doggie style, this is another primal position that will allow him to reach in front and grab any part of your body that he pleases. Or if you'll allow it, he can grab your hair and bring out his inner caveman.

Why you'll love it too:

The Bendover is a great deal less intimate than the Bodyguard position. That said, it's not such a bad idea to bring out your wild side from time to time. While making love, you can guide his hands to your front so he can fondle your breasts or play with your clitoris.

How to do it right:

- Basically, all you need to do is to assume the Bodyguard position first.

- Then, once he's in, simply lean over while stretching your arms out. Do this until your hands are able to come in contact with the floor.

- While your hubby is thrusting in and out of you, you may choose to meet his trusts by pushing back up against him or to just let him take control.

- Balance yourself with your arms and with your hands close to your feet.

Chapter 3

Best Sex Positions for Her

➢ **Spooning Position**

Why your wife will love it:

For most women, sex is all about the romance and the intimacy. The spooning position provides your wife with a feeling of safety. This position also creates a snug fit in a woman's vagina so she'll feel that you're bigger. Your wifey will get more stimulation in the vaginal wall. It's also a great position for slow sex during lazy afternoons.

Why you'll love it too:

Apart from the tighter fit, this is the perfect remedy for morning wood! Wake up in the morning, roll over towards your wife's side of the bed, and make a connection. Sure, this position is not meant for deep penetration but it will allow you to reach into the front and stroke her bits. You can also whisper naughty words to your mate.

How to do it right:

- While facing the same way, both you and your wife should lie on your sides.

- Position yourself behind her and enter her gently from behind. You're wife's gonna have to bring her top leg slightly forward to ease your entry. Likewise, you'll need to lean over a little.

- Wrap your arms around your wife for added intimacy.

- If you want to add more power to your thrusts, grab the top side of your wife's waist.

> **Butterfly Position**

Why your wife will love it:

With this position, your penis will come directly in contact with her upper vaginal walls. This means your wife will get major G-spot stimulation leading to multiple orgasms. More than that, this position promotes intimacy through eye contact. It's also a good position for verbal and non-verbal communication during intercourse.

Why you'll love it too:

Apart from the fact that you'll be giving your wifey multiple O's, this modified missionary position places you in a power position, allowing you to control the pace of lovemaking.

How to do it right:

- Ask your wife to lie on her back. Her hips should be positioned close to the edge of your bed.

- Assume a standing position at the foot of the bed. Then, lift her hips upwards.

- Allow your wife to rest her thighs on your chest. Meanwhile, lay her calves on either side of your shoulders. Alternatively, you can have her legs wrapped around your waist.

- If you want to make your thrusts more vigorous, grab her thighs.

> **Criss Cross Position**

Why your wife will love it:

The Criss Cross provides women with maximum clitoral stimulation.

Why you'll love it too:

This position creates a tighter feel. Even when you're not on top, it's still a dominant position where you're able to control the thrusts. More than that, it allows deeper, more powerful strokes.

How to do it right:

- This position can be done on the bed or a on a table.

- Have your wife lie down on her back. Then, lift her legs so that they are pointing skyward.

- Then, stand up straight and penetrate her. While doing so, your wife should make sure that her legs are straight.

- Help your wife cross her legs at her ankles. After doing this, you'll immediately feel the tighter fit. The more she crosses her legs, the tighter her vagina will feel.

- Alternate your thrusts from deep and hard to quick and shallow.

> **Lotus Position**

Why your wife will love it:

The Lotus is the most intimate sexual position ever invented, dating back from ancient times. In tantra, this is known as a sacred sex position that enables man and wife to connect not just physically but also emotionally and spiritually while having intercourse. This position requires you to look at each other face to face so you can maintain eye contact during sex or engage in deep and passionate kisses.

Why you'll love it too:

Apart from the fact that you'll feel closer to your significant other, this provides your wife easy access to your back. She can provide you with an erotic back rub while making love to you. This is also a good position if you enjoy having your ears and your neck licked.

How to do it right:

- Assume a cross-legged sitting position on bed. You may also choose to do this on the floor or on any flat surface. Just imagine that you're about to do yoga.

- Then, ask your wife to lower herself onto you while facing you.

- Her arms and her legs should end up wrapped around your body.

- Do the same thing and envelop her in your arms.

- Your wife will then make back and forth rocking movements.

- As she does this, kiss your wife's neck and gaze into her face. Whisper some loving words to her. You can tell her how lovely she looks or how good it feels making love to her.

➢ **Pearly Gates Position**

Why your wife will love it:

This is a position that will make your wife feel exposed. Nevertheless, she'll love it. She'll like the sense of abandon that this position will provide her with. Because it's somewhat similar to the spooning position, she'll also feel a sense of security and intimacy.

Why you'll love it too:

This is a simple yet inventive position that's rarely done by couples in bed. Furthermore, it'll give you easy access to her front side if you want to masturbate her while entering her from behind.

How to do it right:

- The two of you should lie on the bed while facing the same way.

- Make sure that your knees are bent and that your feet are flat on the bed.

- Ask your wife to lie on her back on top of you. It's just like spooning but the difference is you're both looking upward.

- Assist your wife in balancing herself. Put your arms around her waist or her chest. Ask her to spread out her arms and her legs.

- Then, keeping your feet flat on the bed, thrust into her. You can also reach in front of your wife to give her a hand, so to speak.

- Make this lovemaking position more intimate by kissing her neck and uttering words of affection into your wife's ear.

Chapter 4

Why Couples Lose their Sex Drive and How to Fix It

There used to be a time when you can't seem to get your hands off each other. But now, whenever one of you wants to have sex, the other's almost always not up for it. Perhaps you still love each other. That much hasn't changed. So what happened? Is it possible to get all "sexed out"?

Before you allow feelings or resentment or guilt to creep into your marriage, you need to understand that there are many factors that affect your libido. These influences range from the kind of job that you have to the stuff that you pop into your mouth. The good news is these factors are modifiable.

> ➢ **Physical Exhaustion**

Most couples wake up early in the morning, go to work, come home, fix dinner, and by the time they hit the sack, they're just plumb tired, not just physically but mentally as well.

The solution? If you want to achieve more O's then you'd better get more Z's first. Lack of sleep diminishes your libido. Try having sex in the morning. Wake up, gargle, and then get it on. You'll observe that sexy time after a good night's rest is so much better than forcing yourselves to do it before bedtime.

➢ Your Hormones are Messed Up

If you're suffering from hormonal imbalances, then it's no wonder your libido has gone loco. Once a woman hits her 40's , she'll experience a decrease in her estrogen levels. This can subsequently lower her libido. More than that, low estrogen levels cause her vagina to dry up, making intercourse painful.

It's not just menopausal women who experience this problem. Individuals with underactive thyroid may possess low sex drives as well. Furthermore, women who use certain types of hormonal contraceptives claim to experience loss of libido.

The solution? Lube up! There are endless variations of lubricants to suit the needs and preferences of different couples. You may also talk to your doctor about hormone replacement therapy to determine whether it's for you. If you suspect that hormonal contraceptives are the cause of your waning sex drive, then you'll need to discuss it with your GP and look for possible family planning alternatives.

➢ You're Not Drinking Enough Water

Dehydration can kill your libido not to mention cause downstairs dryness in women. Men, on the other hand, end up having low sperm counts.

The solution? Rehydrate.

➢ You're Drinking Too Much Alcohol

While a little bit of alcohol can put you in the mood, it can prevent women from achieving orgasm. Likewise, it causes several sexual difficulties in men ranging from erectile dysfunction to ejaculatory problems. Additionally, excessive alcohol consumption causes dehydration.

The solution? Limit alcoholic drinks to two glasses before having sex. (Or less if you have poor alcohol tolerance)

➤ You Sleep With Your Phone

Ideally, the bedroom should be a gadget-free zone. Unless we're talking sex toys. It's easy to get sucked into the world of social media or sports or show business if you bring your laptop to bed. The same can be said about T.V. shows. Keep on with this habit and it'll become more and more difficult for you to think about, much less initiate, sexual intercourse.

The solution? Turn your bedroom into your very own sensual shrine. The bedroom should only be used for two reasons: snoozing and sexing. Thus, bringing work to bed is a big no-no. More than that, remove everything that will remind you of work or chores. Paperwork, shopping lists, and bills don't belong in the bedroom.

Keep in mind that great sex involves all the senses. Use dim lighting. Play relaxing music. Increase your libido by lighting scented candles or incense. Scents that can arouse your wife include vanilla, patchouli, and musk. Scents that can arouse your husband include pumpkin spice, lavender, and citrus.

➤ Your Meds Are Ruining Your Sexual Appetite

As people age, the prescriptions just seem to pile up. Certain anti-depressants, drugs for heartburn, and medication for hypertension can decrease your sex drive.

The solution? Check with your doctor if any of your prescribed meds have libido-lowering side effects. If yes, talk about alternatives.

> ➤ **It's Just the Same Ol' Same Ol'**

Getting into a sex rut is a number one libido killer. It's inevitable for couples who have been together for so long to form a routine that they're comfortable with. But when things get too predictable, there's just nothing more to look forward to. You've already stripped away the mystery and the only way to make up for it is through variety. Switch things up before your partner starts looking for excitement elsewhere.

The solution? Communication. Sit with your spouse and talk about your deepest (even your darkest) desires. Listen to each other in a non-judgmental way. Compromise. Let each other know what you're willing to try. If your partner's fantasies turn out to be a little too much for you, rather than saying "No.", simply say "Not yet." Because hey, you'll never know... Give and take. Make sure that you exercise fairness on considering each other's carnal wishes.

> ➤ **You Wouldn't Even Dare Sleep With Yourself**

Have you looked at yourself in the mirror lately? How well have you been taking care of yourself? When people age, they gain weight, their skin loses its elasticity, and other undesirable changes occur. The less attractive you feel, the lower your libido becomes. This decreases your confidence in the bedroom, causing you to shy away from intimacy.

The solution? Take care of yourself. More than just maintaining proper hygiene, prep your body for sex by shaving your legs/nether regions or wearing underwear that makes you feel sexy. More importantly, boost each other's confidence. Give each other sincere compliments. Don't be afraid to tell your partner what you love most about him/her. Kiss that body part frequently. If your partner has made an effort to look more appealing in bed (even if it's as simple as spraying on some perfume), make sure that you let him/her know that you've noticed and appreciate it. Make an effort to look good and do it together. Help each other to age gracefully. Exercise together. Eat healthy together. Bathe each other.

Chapter 5

How to Maintain a Great Sex Life: More Tips from Real Happy Couples

> ➢ **Make a sex jar.**

If you can make a Christmas list, then you sure as hell can make a bucket list for sex. Write down all of your hottest fantasies on small pieces of paper and throw them in your sex jar. You can fill the jar with anything from new sexual positions that you'd like to try to exotic places that you'd like to have sex in. Each time you're feeling adventurous, pick a paper from the jar and just do what it says. If you can't do it then and there, set a date.

> ➢ **Incorporate food with sex.**

Before making love, feed each other aphrodisiacs like strawberries or oysters. Pour chocolate syrup or ice cream into each other's bodies and lick it off. Better yet, turn your body into an aphrodisiac buffet by adorning yourself with grapes, cucumber slices, etc. and invite your spouse to feast on you.

> ➢ **Formulate your own codes for sex.**

Make a gesture or a word for sex that only the both of you will understand. Tease each other in public. Foreplay doesn't necessarily have to happen immediately prior to sex. It can start as early as before he/she leaves for work in the morning. You can leave a sexy note in his/her briefcase/purse or even leave handcuffs in his/her car. Communicate through subtle signs and sexy glances over dinner to increase each other's anticipation for "dessert"!

> **Try no-orgasm sex.**

Yes, you read it right. Couples make the mistake of treating orgasm as the end-all and be-all of sexual intercourse. From time to time, try to just connect with each other... feeling each other, being one with each other, and taking your time. This may take some getting used to but once you get the hang of it, you'll realize how it can actually strengthen your bond and deepen your intimacy.

> **Alter your evening routine.**

When you follow a certain routine every evening, it's easy to just get comfortable and fall asleep. Shaking up your repertoire (ex. feeding each other dessert, playing a game, etc.) can open up other possibilities apart from sleep.

> **Get naked more often.**

This opens up the possibility for more frequent sex. Sleeping in the nude can actually bring about sexier wet dreams that will help get you in the mood.

> **Have sex one day before her period arrives.**

Sounds weird? The accumulation of blood causes her uterus to be heavy. Because of this, contractions become more intense during orgasm. More than that, during this time, her clitoris and her labia become more sensitive.

➢ Play with each other.

Rigorous activity before sex releases feel good chemicals in your body. So go out on a run, take a few laps, chase each other around the bedroom, or just tickle each other in bed.

➢ Masturbate with each other.

Or engage in non-intercourse sex. Apart from the fact that you will be providing each other with a visual delight, it'll be like taking each other back to the good ol' days when you were young and not quite ready to have sex yet. Talk about a sexy blast from the past!

➢ Explore each other's erogenous zones.

Don't just limit yourself to pleasuring your partner's genitalia. Caress, kiss, and lick each other's hot spots such as the nape of the neck, the ears, the back, and the inner thighs. Men should pay more attention to their wives' sacrum. Likewise, women should explore their husbands' perineum.

➢ Experiment with tantric sex.

If it worked for the royals of ancient times, then it might be worth checking out, right? Learn some new moves from the wisdom of the past. Tantric sex is all about prolonging each other's pleasure to give each other powerful orgasms. But more than that, it's also about deepening your connection in the physical, emotional, mental, and spiritual level. That's the way sex in marriage is supposed to be.

Sex:

Make her beg for more and be the best she's ever been with in bed!

Introduction

Are you looking to bring your sex up a notch?

Throughout this book you will learn common killers of arousal and how to prevent them. Sex is exciting and should always be exciting. This book shows you how to always do that.

Here is a synopsis of what you will learn:

-Common killers of erection

-Best techniques to maintain a strong erection and orgasm

-Best sex positions for orgasm

-Oral sex and handplay

Chapter 1 – Why Your Erection is limp:

A lack of an erection is always caused by a lack of blood flow to the penis. This lack of blood flow can be caused by a variety of issues. Erectile dysfunction is not a question of age and something that only older men have to worry about-as it can be prevalent in younger men too. According to *The Journal of Sexual Medicine,* about 25% of men under 40 experience erectile dysfunction and are actively seeking help about it.

Here are many of the likely causes behind the lack of an erection:

You're watching too much Porn:

While we all watch porn (whether we want to admit it or not), too much porn can actually be detrimental to your sex life. This is so because the brain-not your penis-is the problem. Too much porn watching, starting at age 14, and daily viewing up until the mid 20s-causes desensitization in the penis. Essentially, your brain is getting used to even the most raunchy sex acts as a result of watching too much porn. Therefore, your penis is losing libido and an inability to maintain an erection.

Real life sex is different from porn sex. You and your partner might be engaging in normal sexual activity versus the threesomes, gangbangs, bdsm, etc. that you see in porn.

The solution: Watch less porn. Over a period of several months of minimal porn exposure will desensitize certain receptors in the brain. Additionally-touching and being with your partner more often while conversely watching less porn can help immensely. More intimacy with your partner and less with the computer screen are key.

Anxiety:

Men suffer from anxiety just as much as women. Anxiety can seriously lower libido and mess with the nervous system-leading to a lack of an erection. Stress at work, overworking and overcommitting oneself are common causes of this.

The solution: We can write an entire book on confidence and conquering anxiety-but that's bot what this book is about. However, it is important that you eliminate any unnecessary stressors in your life-whether they be at work or at home. Saying no to things, people, and commitments can solve this. Getting a solid 8 hours of rest each night can help this too. Don't allow yourself to be stressed out too often. Not only this is bad for your health-but it kills your sex life as well.

Unhealthy Habits: Smoking, malnutrition, lack of exercise, and alcoholism are all major contributors. These are likely the biggest culprits. If you are looking for an excuse to get healthy-then this is it.

The solution: Limit your smoking and drinking habits to sparing use weekly. Exercise at least 4-5 times a week and take care of yourself.

There are good solutions that can address these problems. Men with erectile dysfunction can benefit from erectile disorder medications such as Cialis, Viagra, or Levitra. This restores confidence, and also makes sex relatively worry free.

However, in general the biggest culprit to erectile dysfunction are the lifestyle habits aforementioned. Taking care of your eating/exercise habits, managing stress well, and keeping most of the arousal between you and your partner (and not some girls on the computer screen!) are key.

Chapter 2 – How to get harder-for longer:

How do you increase the stamina of your erections? Very few treatments and devices that claim to help out with erections hold much water. However, most of the time you can improve your erections by your actions and your choices alone.

Here are some great tips on how to maintain a stronger and more powerful erection:

Eat healthy and exercise:

We stated this before-but this is huge. Difficult to digest foods that are bad for you kill your energy and ruin your libido. Lack of exercise decreases blood flow to the penis. Eat healthy and exercise regularly, as these maintain strong energy levels within you and you will notice a huge difference.

Abdominal exercises are great for erections. Abdominal muscles support and maintain your erections-so therefore ab exercises will make you harder. Also-you don't want to have sex with a large gut anyways.

Check out Kegel exercises as well. These are great for erections. Kegel exercises are considered the best exercises for sex drive.

Be in proper position:

A man that is on top or is in a standing sex position has great blood flow to his penis. When you feel your erection needs a boost during sex changing your position can make a difference. Any sex position where you are on top will give you a natural advantage.

Wear a condom:

When you wear a condom-you are limiting sensitivity and therefore are helping yourself maintain a longer erection. You should be wearing a condom anyways most of the time. Wearing a condom loosens the sensitivity and therefore delays ejaculation from coming too early.

Be mindful of any medications you are taking:

Any type of medication can be a major boner-killer if used in an improper dose. Work with your doctor on making sure you are taking the right dosages and nothing more. It is unfortunate that a lot of medications are sex killers and significantly decrease your libido.

Don't Masturbate too much:

As they always say-too much of anything isn't good for you. Neither is too much masturbation. This is similar to watching too much porn. You want to make sure that you are saving your arousal and libido mostly for Miss Right and not Mr. Right Hand.

Communicate to each other about your wildest sex fantasies:

Check out my book titled "Spice Up Your Sex Life" for more information about this-as this book goes over common fantasies between men and women regarding sex. But in summary-there are always more ways to make your sex life more fun and more kinky. You don't want to do the "same old, same old" all the time-as that creates a routine and reduces arousal and libido and excitement for sex. Be honest and open to each other and don't be afraid to get kinky!

Talk Dirty:

I wrote two books on this subject (one for men, one for women)-but to summarize-simply saying dirty phrases such as "Let me fuck your wet juicy pussy all night long", "I want you to ride my hard throbbing cock", "Let me cum all over your face and tits," "I'm gonna lick your asshole and pussy all night long", are all arousing phrases that can really put someone in the mood for sex. Foreplay like this is critical!

Read Erotica Novels with your partner:

Again, this is one of the things that I touch on in my book "Spice Up Your Sex Life". This is a great way to come up with some naughty ideas on how to come up with more kinky techniques for the bedroom.

Get out of your head:

Stay in the moment when having sex. If your mind is wandering and asking unnecessary questions and thoughts-then you will kill the fun. Focus on pleasing your partner and having fun!

Chapter 3 – Best Sex positions for Orgasm

Now that we've gone over why you are having trouble maintaining an erection, we are going to talk about how to help her get a peak orgasm. We are also going to talk about top sex positions as well.

Here are some tips:

Touch your perineum:

The perineum is located between a woman's pussy and butt, and between a man's penis/balls and butt. Touching and caressing each other in that area is a great way for massive pleasure. The perineum is extremely sensitive-as there are a lot of nerves in that area. Having multiple ejaculations and orgasms is very possible with enough pressure and attention to the perineum. Give this area the attention it deserves. Ask your partner to place a finger there and press feels awesome.

Engage in kegels exercises:

For both men and women-kegels exercises work out the muscles around the penis and vagina. Give these a try! This is known as the one exercise that can save your sex life!

Breathe right:

Breathe slowly and naturally will improve oxygen and bloodflow to your penis or pussy. Be mindful of your breathing pattern. This is talked about a lot during tantric sex. Climax is strengthened with proper breathing.

Use sex toys:

Vibrators, strap-on penises, butt plugs, dildos, etc. are all awesome additions to your sex life and can give it a boost.

Delay gratification:

Show this tip to your woman. Good things come to those who wait! When your woman is about 95% of the way towards orgasm-have her stop herself.....she is essentially building herself up for a bigger and better orgasm. Continuously building up and pausing, building up and pausing, will build up to an explosive orgasm at the end leaving her squirting and cumming all over the place.

Now that we've gone over some basic tips-lets talk about the best sex positions for both genders:

Best Sex Positions for Him (have your wife/girlfriend read this section-as this is for her!)

Doggie Style:

Why he'll love it

Generally, men love rear-entry positions because they place them in a position of control. This means that he can regulate the thrusts, to slow it down or speed it up depending on what works best for him. The doggie style is a very primal position and such positions make him feel very manly.

Furthermore, this sex position allows deep penetration so this makes him feel like he's giving you all that he's got and likewise, he's taking all that you have. Additionally, he gets a great view of your butt.

Why you'll love it too

This position can provide you with a full sensation that's really intense.

How to do it right

- First, you'll need to get down on your hands and on your knees.

- Make sure that your legs are spread slightly apart.

- Your man will then get down on his knees and then enter you from the butt. He may either place his hands on your back or he may grab your waist if he wants to perform harder thrusts. Alternatively, he may hold on to your shoulders. Or if you're in the mood for rough sex, allow him to grab your hair.

- If you want your man to go deeper into you, meet his thrusts by pushing your backside against him.

- If you want to change angles, you may lower your body onto the ground.

- You may also make use of your free hand to stimulate your pussy. Or you may take your man's hand and guide it towards your love button.

- Maintaining this position can be a bit problematic on your part unless you've got great arm strength. Here's a valuable tip: Try performing this position on the floor by the bed. This way, you can remove your weight off your hands and rest the upper part of your body.

Cowgirl Position:

Why your man will love it

Most men wish their wives/girlfriends would do Woman on Top positions more often. Nobody wants a passive partner in bed. But more than that, one of your man's primary goals during sex is to please you. Knowing that he is able to satisfy you physically boosts his ego. Additionally, the cowgirl position provides him with a full view of your body. Remember, men are very visual creatures.

Why you'll love it too

This position can provide you with a sense of empowerment. Being on top will allow you to regulate the pace, depending on what you think works best for you. More importantly, this ensures that his penis hits all your right spots. Thus, your chances of achieving orgasm in this position ranges from huge to inevitable.

Furthermore, if you'd like to tease your man or prolong his pleasure, this power position can help you do that.

How to do it right

- Your man should be lying on his back.

- Afterwards, you'll have to straddle him while you are kneeling. Make sure that your legs are situated on either side of your man's waist.

- Insert his cock into your pussy. It is recommended you either suck or play with his cock first to make sure he is really hard. Move yourself up and down. If you want to adjust the angle, do this by simply leaning forward or backward. Doing so will provide more stimulation for your clit and your outer vagina.

- You may choose to rest your hands on your hubby's chest. To maintain intimacy during sex, it's best to remain in contact with whatever body part you can get hold of. That's the other advantage of this position. It allows eye contact between you and your partner so lovemaking becomes more intimate.

- Try having sex in this position with the lights on. This way, he can see your curves. Let go of your feelings of self-consciousness. Also, since your man gets a full view of your face, drive him mad by biting your lip or with sexy facial expressions. You're in the spotlight so put on a show!

Reverse Cowgirl Position:

Why your man will love it

He'll love it for the simple reason that it gives him an awesome view of your butt.

Why you'll love it too

You'll love this for the same reasons that you'll love the cowgirl position. The difference is that this'll keep your frontal curves hidden from your hubby's view. This one's a recommended baby step if you're not ready to get past your feelings of self-consciousness.

How to do it right

- First, ask your hubby to lie on his back.

- Then, assume a kneeling position and with your back to him, straddle your man. Your knees must be on either side of his body.

- Insert his cock into your pussy again. Perform the trusts by moving up and down, slow or fast or alternate.

- If you want to adjust the angle, just lean backward or forward.

- If you want to switch things up a bit, try making slow grinding maneuvers with your hips.

Bodyguard Position:

Why your man will love it

This is basically just a classic standing position. Men tend to love it because it's perfect for let's-fuck-here-and-now moments. This is something that you can do when you're standing by the sink in the kitchen or in cramped rooms when you sneak off for an afternooner. Furthermore, by holding on to your waist, he'll be able to perform harder, deeper thrusts. With this position, the mood can easily change from romantic to rough.

Why you'll love it too

Even though it's a position for quickies, the Bodyguard isn't necessarily devoid of intimacy. With your back pressed against his front, your man can nibble on your ear, kiss your neck, or whisper sweet, sexy words while having sex.

How to do it right

- Begin with the both of you standing upright. You should both be facing the same direction.

- Then, grab your man's penis and insert it into either your butt or pussy from behind.

- Meet his thrusts by pushing your body back onto his.

Bendover Position:

Why your man will love it

This is another rear-entry standing position that's perfect for quickies. Much like the doggie style, this is another primal position that will allow him to reach in front and grab any part of your body that he pleases. Or if you'll allow it, he can grab your hair and bring out his inner caveman.

Why you'll love it too

The Bendover is a great deal less intimate than the Bodyguard position. That said, it's not such a bad idea to bring out your wild side from time to time. While making love, you can guide his hands to your front so he can fondle your boobs or play with your clit.

How to do it right

- Basically, all you need to do is to assume the Bodyguard position first.

- Then, once his cock is in you, simply lean over while stretching your arms out. Do this until your hands are able to come in contact with the floor.

- While your hubby is thrusting in and out of you, you may choose to meet his trusts by pushing back up against him or to just let him take control.

- Balance yourself with your arms and with your hands close to your feet.

Best Sex Positions for Her

Spooning Position:

Why your woman will love it

For most women, sex is all about the romance and the intimacy. The spooning position provides your woman with a feeling of safety. This position also makes her pussy tighter so she'll feel that you're bigger. Your woman will get more stimulation in the vaginal wall. It's also a great position for slow sex during lazy afternoons.

Why you'll love it too

Apart from the tighter fit, this is the perfect remedy for morning wood! Wake up in the morning, roll over towards your woman's side of the bed, and make a connection. Sure, this position is not meant for deep penetration but it will allow you to reach into the front and stroke her bits. You can also whisper naughty words to your mate.

How to do it right

- While facing the same way, both you and your woman should lie on your sides.

- Position yourself behind her and enter her gently from behind. You're woman's gonna have to bring her top leg slightly forward to ease your entry. Likewise, you'll need to lean over a little.

- Wrap your arms around your woman and fondle her tits for added intimacy.

- If you want to add more power to your thrusts, grab the top side of your woman's waist.

Butterfly Position:

Why your woman will love it

With this position, your penis will come directly in contact with her upper vaginal walls. This means your woman will get major G-spot stimulation leading to multiple orgasms. More than that, this position promotes intimacy through eye contact. It's also a good position for verbal and non-verbal communication during intercourse.

Why you'll love it too

Apart from the fact that you'll be giving your woman multiple O's, this modified missionary position places you in a power position, allowing you to control the pace of lovemaking.

How to do it right:

- Ask your woman to lie on her back. Her hips should be positioned close to the edge of your bed.

- Assume a standing position at the foot of the bed. Then, lift her hips upwards.

- Allow your woman to rest her thighs on your chest. Meanwhile, lay her calves on either side of your shoulders. Alternatively, you can have her legs wrapped around your waist.

- If you want to make your thrusts more vigorous, grab her thighs.

Criss Cross Position:

Why your woman will love it

The Criss Cross provides women with maximum clitoral stimulation.

Why you'll love it too

This position creates a tighter feel. Even when you're not on top, it's still a dominant position where you're able to control the thrusts. More than that, it allows deeper, more powerful strokes.

How to do it right:

- This position can be done on the bed or a on a table.

- Have your woman lie down on her back. Then, lift her legs so that they are pointing skyward.

- Then, stand up straight and penetrate her. While doing so, your woman should make sure that her legs are straight.

- Help her cross her legs at her ankles. After doing this, you'll immediately feel the tighter fit. The more she crosses her legs, the tighter her pussy will feel.

- Alternate your thrusts from deep and hard to quick and shallow.

Lotus Position:

Why your woman will love it

The Lotus is the most intimate sexual position ever invented, dating back from ancient times. In tantra, this is known as a sacred sex position that enables man and woman to connect not just physically but also emotionally and spiritually while having intercourse. This position requires you to look at each other face to face so you can maintain eye contact during sex or engage in deep and passionate kisses.

Why you'll love it too

Apart from the fact that you'll feel closer to your significant other, this provides your woman easy access to your back. She can provide you with an erotic back rub while making love to you. This is also a good position if you enjoy having your ears and your neck licked.

How to do it right

- Assume a cross-legged sitting position on bed. You may also choose to do this on the floor or on any flat surface. Just imagine that you're about to do yoga.

- Then, ask your woman to lower herself onto you while facing you.

- Her arms and her legs should end up wrapped around your body.

- Do the same thing and envelop her in your arms.

- Your woman will then make back and forth rocking movements.

- As she does this, kiss your woman's neck and gaze into her face. Whisper some loving words to her. You can tell her how lovely she looks or how good it feels making love to her.

Pearly Gates Position:

Why your woman will love it

This is a position that will make your woman feel exposed. Nevertheless, she'll love it. She'll like the sense of abandon that this position will provide her with. Because it's somewhat similar to the spooning position, she'll also feel a sense of security and intimacy.

Why you'll love it too

This is a simple yet inventive position that's rarely done by couples in bed. Furthermore, it'll give you easy access to her front side if you want to masturbate her while entering her from behind.

How to do it right

- The two of you should lie on the bed while facing the same way.

- Make sure that your knees are bent and that your feet are flat on the bed.

- Ask your woman to lie on her back on top of you. It's just like spooning but the difference is you're both looking upward.

- Assist your woman in balancing herself. Put your arms around her waist or her chest. Ask her to spread out her arms and her legs.

- Put your cock into her butt or pussy. Then, keeping your feet flat on the bed, thrust into her. You can also reach in front of your woman to give her a hand, so to speak.

- Make this lovemaking position more intimate by kissing her neck and uttering words of affection into your woman's ear.

Chapter 4 – Best Oral Sex Techniques for Men

Lets talk about eating pussy. Cuninglus on your woman's vagina is one of sexiest part of sexual intercourse. If done right, oral sex can make a woman orgasm alone. The best way to go about this is through some trial and error to see what turns her on.

Lets talk about a couple obstacles about oral sex first:

The hairy pussy:

A little bit of a bush on her vagina isn't such a bad thing. However, in general most guys like a well groomed pussy-as a hairy bush creates a barrier for oral sex. A full Brazilian wax along with regular shaving can prevent this. If your woman has a bush barrier, encourage her to continue to shave her pubes. Otherwise it will limit her ability to be pleased by you!

The Unfresh pussy:

After a long day of work, dinner, and putting the kids to bed.... It is understandable for your woman to be hesitant to let your face near her pussy and butt. As I always recommend-always shower before having sex. It leaves a nice fresh feeling down there.

Now that we've talked about a couple of obstacles, its time to give some more tips on giving oral to your woman:

Use a pillow:

Put a pillow under her butt. This raised her pelvis higher and presents her pussy better. This will allow for better G-spot stimulation.

Use your hands:

Grab her buttcheeks while you are driving your tongue into her pussylips. This intensifies the feeling. Giving oral without using your hands properly is just awkward. You can also finger fuck her from the bottom of her pussy while licking her at the same time.

Tease her:

Gradually build up. Going for the pussy right away is too soon, too fast. Instead, as I always say-incorporate some foreplay first. Several minutes of groping, fingering and making out are a great way to start. You can also kiss and lick her inner thighs several inches from her vagina. This area is very sensitive and is a huge turn on.

Spit on it!

A sexy thing to do before you give your woman oral is to spit on her pussy. Massage her pussy and rub the saliva all over the lips of her vagina. This makes her pussy juicier. You can also do this to her perineum and butthole as well.

Here are some popular oral sex positions:

Doggy goes oral:

This position is essentially face down, ass up. This is a hot position because it gives you a nice spread out view of her pussy and butthole. You have a great opportunity to lick both her pussy and her butthole, as well as her perineum. Kiss her pussy, kiss her buttcheeks, finger her ass.... Use your imagination!

The Cliffhanger:

For this position, have her lay on the bed on her back with her legs over the edge of the bed. Make sure she has her legs spread apart so you can access her pussy. This position is great because not only can you give her oral, but you can reach and fondle her tits as well.

The Southern Exposure:

This is when your woman lies on the bed on her back, lifts her feet and legs in the air and spreads her pussy and butthole open. This gives you, like the "Doggy goes oral" position to make love to her pussy, perineum and butt.

The 69:

Most people know this one, but this might be the best position. While you are lying on your back-have her "sit on your face" so her pussy is on your mouth, and then bend over until she can reach and place your cock in her mouth. Give each other oral and eat her out!

Standing up:

This is where your woman stands up and opens her legs just enough so you can have access to her pussy. Devour her pussy in this position and squeeze her buttcheeks while you're at it. You can also do this in reverse direction-where her butt is in your face. Have her spread her legs open enough and spread her buttcheeks open so you can eat away! You can also perform analingus in this position as well.

Now that we've talked about some basic pussy-licking techniques... lets talk about fingering!

Make sure your nails are groomed:

You don't want to hurt her on the inside because of a sharp fingernail!!

Only touch a woman's private parts when she is aroused:

As I've said before-make sure you've done some foreplay first. It feels awkward fingering her when she hasn't gotten aroused yet.

Move slowly:

Gradually kiss her inner thighs, her perineum, and gently rub her clitoris with one finger. Then slowly move towards kissing her pussylips. Afterwards, slowly enter 1 finger into her pussy. Then move to two fingers or more. The key though is to move slowly.

Focus on your partner:

While her pussy may be beautiful-keep talking to her and looking at her in the eyes. In the end its about love.

Find the right spot:

The G-spot is on her vaginal walls. Once you have both fingers in her, keep rubbing her vaginal walls. Look at her face when doing this. You will know when you've found the G-spot based off of her excited facial expressions.

Chapter 5-How to give her a rim job

If you don't know what a rim job/rimming or analingus are-it is the art of sucking, caressing, and licking your partner's butthole. For obvious reasons-this can be gross if done wrong. However, if done properly this can be extremely sexy, as it is easy to have a peak experience when your butthole is being attacked. The butthole is a sensitive area!

Rimming is not for everyone. But to many watching a clean and fit woman having her asshole licked is a hot and steamy thing. Imagine a hot, wet, naked model such as Kate Upton walking out of the shower. You'd want to lick every inch of her, including all over her butt!

The butthole has a ton of nerve endings, which is why analingus can be so sexy. Women will be surprised with how much they like it if they have never tried it before. So give it a try!

Here are some tips on rimming:

Shower first!

The first tip with analingus is to make sure you and your partner have both showered beforehand (as you always should before sex). The reason is obvious-as the anus is the area of most concern regarding hygiene. However-as long as you and your partner have showered and have washed each others' genitals well analingus should be fun.

Foreplay is a must!

Just walking up to your woman and immediately sucking and licking on her butthole won't work for peak experience. Shoving your tongue up her ass is only half the battle.

Communicate through dirty talk or intimacy beforehand to build up the anticipation.

On her back, legs spread open:

This is one way you can perform analingus. While your naked woman is lying on her back with her legs spread wide open is a great opportunity to eat her pussy. Finger, caress, and lick her pussy first. This alone should turn her on. Then, while licking her pussy take one or two of your fingers and gently move them in circles on and around her butthole. This will build up anticipation. Kiss, nibble, and lick her perineum (the area between her butt and her pussy). Finally, surprise her by lifting her buttcheeks up and giving her an aggressive tongue attack up her butthole. Switching between aggressively licking her butthole and slowly/passionately licking and kissing her butthole will drive her absolutely crazy. While you are performing analingus, massage her clit in small circles.

Face down, ass up:

This is the second major method on where analingus is performed, where your woman is on her hands and knees with her legs spread out and her butt and pussy are in your face. Begin by licking her pussy from behind and gently finger fuck her at the same time. Then, you can alternate from pussylicking to kissing her buttcheeks and then slowly making it to kissing her butthole. Once you start moving your mouth towards her butthole, make sure you continue to finger and caress her vagina. Be sure to kiss and nibble on the perineum as well. Finally, start licking and sucking on her butthole and cheeks. Spitting on her butthole and using your fingers to rub the saliva around her butthole and pussy is a great sexy addition to this.

This method is more effective than the first-as her butthole and pussy are both well exposed and you can do more with both with your hands and mouth. However, do whatever position is most comfortable for both you and your partner.

Lick her pussy first, and then her butthole:

If you first perform analingus and then lick her vagina afterwards-you are putting her at risk of transferring bacteria from the butthole to her clit. This can result in an infection.

Use a vibrator:

While giving her a rim job, using a vibrator in her pussy is a huge turn on. She will lose her mind over this because she is getting stimulation from two areas at once!

Use buttplugs:

Other methods of anal play involved toys such as butt plugs. While you are eating her pussy you can play with her butt with a buttplug too-if rim jobs are not for you.

Sex:

The Hottest Tips for Better Orgasms!

Introduction

Are you looking to bring your sex up a notch?

Throughout this book you will learn common killers of arousal and how to prevent them. Sex is exciting and should always be exciting. This book shows you how to always do that.

Here is a synopsis of what you will learn:

-Common killers of orgasm

-Best techniques to maintain orgasm

-Best sex positions for orgasm

-Oral sex and handplay

-How to give a rim job

Chapter 1 – Why you can't orgasm

The truth is..... you need to own your own orgasm. Sometimes you get in your own way of your sex drive.

Here are a number of reasons why you aren't having strong orgasms:

You don't have enough foreplay:

Letting your man get in your pussy too easy is not good for orgasm. Do not rush through foreplay. Just like a runner needs to do a 10-15 minute warm-up before a long run-a couple needs to sexually tease each other and build up anticipation before a sex session.

Studies have shown that women need around 20 minutes of arousal time to reach the "orgasmic platform." Skipping the sex-response cycle makes it hard for men to ejaculate and cum and for women to orgasm. In the case of sex, patience pays!

Also-I would recommend you check out my other book on Dirty Talk for Women-but to summarize.... Phrases such as "Pound my little wet pussy", "I want to lick, fuck, and suck your juicy sticky hard throbbing cock", "Bite my tits", or "I'm going to sit on your face and rub my wet pussy in your face" are huge turn-ons and great for foreplay.

You get distracted easily:

Set your environment for the right tone for sex. As they say-the bedroom should be used for two things: sleep and sex. Nothing else allowed and no exceptions. Turn off the t.v. and computer and anything else noisy in the house. Especially be sure to leave your smartphones outside of the room. These distractions can easily kill arousal, as it is psychologically proven that these distractions spark conflicting neurological impulses that weaken sex impulses in the brain and therefore reduce sexual pleasure.

Eliminate all distractions and mental thoughts when having sex. Be 100% present, in the moment, and focusing on having fun and amazing sex with your partner.

You haven't peed before sex:

It is important that you pee before you have sex. When your G-spot is stimulated enough-it will feel like you have to pee and therefore your vagina will clench up. Sometimes during sex women will "squirt" and think that they are urinating when they are in fact releasing ejaculatory fluid. As a result their pussy clenches up and kills their orgasm. Simply take a moment to pee before sex and this will remove the likelihood of this. Any fluid coming out of your vagina during sex will be ejaculatory fluid, and since you are aware you just peed, you will be free to let it go and not clench up.

You're trying too many different sex positions:

It is important to experiment with as many different sex positions as possible with your partner. However-during a single sex session, it is important to focus on a handful of sex positions per session to maintain steady stimulation. Too many sex positions and switching sex positions too often can confuse your brain's focus and cause you to not build up the arousal necessary for a solid hot orgasm.

You're stressed out:

Stress kills libido and sex drive. It is important that you eliminate any unnecessary stressors in your life-whether they be at work or at home. Saying no to things, people, and commitments can solve this. Getting a solid 8 hours of rest each night can help this too. Don't allow yourself to be stressed out too often. Not only this is bad for your health-but it kills your sex life as well.

You're trying too hard:

Thinking too much about having an orgasm can counter intuitively kill your orgasm. This is true because you are telling your brain "Orgasm! Orgasm! Orgasm!"-however you are not focused on the actual sex and being in the present moment. Focus on having an awesome time with your partner and giving and receiving pleasure-not just focusing on orgasm. When your man is penetrating you G-spot or licking your pussy-focus on being relaxed and allowing him to please you, and the stimulation will take care of itself.

You're not being confident enough:

Confidence is important with sex. You need to be willing to lose yourself during sex in order to climax. Loosen up and be yourself. Holding back and having insecurities will kill your sex drive.

Chapter 2 – Best Ways to maintain Orgasm

Now that we've gone over why you are having trouble reaching orgasm, we are going to talk about how to get a peak orgasm. We are also going to talk about top sex positions as well.

Here are some tips:

Touch your perineum:

The perineum is located between a woman's pussy and butt, and between a man's penis/balls and butt. Touching and caressing each other in that area is a great way for massive pleasure. The perineum is extremely sensitive-as there are a lot of nerves in that area. Having multiple ejaculations and orgasms is very possible with enough pressure and attention to the perineum. Give this area the attention it deserves. Ask your partner to place a finger there and press feels awesome.

Engage in kegels exercises:

For both men and women-kegels exercises work out the muscles around the penis and vagina. Give these a try! This is known as the one exercise that can save your sex life!

Know where your G-spot is:

Be willing to guide your man's penis or fingers towards your G-spot. Make sure he's aiming in the right direction.

However, men have an equivalent to the G-spot as well.....the prostate. Anal probing can be sexy. Please read the later chapter on analingus-but anal stimulation is sexy. Put a lubricated finger approximately two inches in your man's butthole. When you find a chestnut-sized lump that feels sensitive...you've found it! Give your man some pressure towards that area and he'll go nuts.

Breathe right:

Breathe slowly and naturally will improve oxygen and blood flow to your penis or pussy. Be mindful of your breathing pattern. This is talked about a lot during tantric sex. Climax is strengthened with proper breathing.

Use sex toys:

Vibrators, strap-on penises, butt plugs, dildos, etc. are all awesome additions to your sex life and can give it a boost.

Delay gratification:

Good things come to those who wait! When you are about 95% of the way towards orgasm and then stop yourself.....you are essentially building yourself up for a bigger and better orgasm. Continuously building up and pausing, building up and pausing, will build up to an explosive orgasm at the end leaving her squirting and cumming all over the place.

Best Sex Positions for Him

Doggie Style:

Why he'll love it

Generally, men love rear-entry positions because they place them in a position of control. This means that he can regulate the thrusts, to slow it down or speed it up depending on what works best for him. The doggie style is a very primal position and such positions make him feel very manly.

Furthermore, this sex position allows deep penetration so this makes him feel like he's giving you all that he's got and likewise, he's taking all that you have. Additionally, he gets a great view of your butt.

Why you'll love it too

This position can provide you with a full sensation that's really intense.

How to do it right

- First, you'll need to get down on your hands and on your knees.

- Make sure that your legs are spread slightly apart.

- Your man will then get down on his knees and then enter you from the butt. He may either place his hands on your back or he may grab your waist if he wants to perform harder thrusts. Alternatively, he may hold on to your shoulders. Or if you're in the mood for rough sex, allow him to grab your hair.

- If you want your man to go deeper into you, meet his thrusts by pushing your backside against him.

- If you want to change angles, you may lower your body onto the ground.

- You may also make use of your free hand to stimulate your pussy. Or you may take your man's hand and guide it towards your love button.

- Maintaining this position can be a bit problematic on your part unless you've got great arm strength. Here's a valuable tip: Try performing this position on the floor by the bed. This way, you can remove your weight off your hands and rest the upper part of your body.

Cowgirl Position:

Why your man will love it

Most men wish their wives/girlfriends would do Woman on Top positions more often. Nobody wants a passive partner in bed. But more than that, one of your man's primary goals during sex is to please you. Knowing that he is able to satisfy you physically boosts his ego. Additionally, the cowgirl position provides him with a full view of your body. Remember, men are very visual creatures.

Why you'll love it too

This position can provide you with a sense of empowerment. Being on top will allow you to regulate the pace, depending on what you think works best for you. More importantly, this ensures that his penis hits all your right spots. Thus, your chances of achieving orgasm in this position ranges from huge to inevitable.

Furthermore, if you'd like to tease your man or prolong his pleasure, this power position can help you do that.

How to do it right

- Your man should be lying on his back.

- Afterwards, you'll have to straddle him while you are kneeling. Make sure that your legs are situated on either side of your man's waist.

- Insert his cock into your pussy. It is recommended you either suck or play with his cock first to make sure he is really hard. Move yourself up and down. If you want to adjust the angle, do this by simply leaning forward or backward. Doing so will provide more stimulation for your clit and your outer vagina.

- You may choose to rest your hands on your hubby's chest. To maintain intimacy during sex, it's best to remain in contact with whatever body part you can get hold of. That's the other advantage of this position. It allows eye contact between you and your partner so lovemaking becomes more intimate.

- Try having sex in this position with the lights on. This way, he can see your curves. Let go of your feelings of self-consciousness. Also, since your man gets a full view of your face, drive him mad by biting your lip or with sexy facial expressions. You're in the spotlight so put on a show!

Reverse Cowgirl Position:

Why your man will love it

He'll love it for the simple reason that it gives him an awesome view of your butt.

Why you'll love it too

You'll love this for the same reasons that you'll love the cowgirl position. The difference is that this'll keep your frontal curves hidden from your hubby's view. This one's a recommended baby step if you're not ready to get past your feelings of self-consciousness.

How to do it right

- First, ask your hubby to lie on his back.

- Then, assume a kneeling position and with your back to him, straddle your man. Your knees must be on either side of his body.

- Insert his cock into your pussy again. Perform the trusts by moving up and down, slow or fast or alternate.

- If you want to adjust the angle, just lean backward or forward.

- If you want to switch things up a bit, try making slow grinding maneuvers with your hips.

Bodyguard Position:

Why your man will love it

This is basically just a classic standing position. Men tend to love it because it's perfect for let's-fuck-here-and-now moments. This is something that you can do when you're standing by the sink in the kitchen or in cramped rooms when you sneak off for an afternooner. Furthermore, by holding on to your waist, he'll be able to perform harder, deeper thrusts. With this position, the mood can easily change from romantic to rough.

Why you'll love it too

Even though it's a position for quickies, the Bodyguard isn't necessarily devoid of intimacy. With your back pressed against his front, your man can nibble on your ear, kiss your neck, or whisper sweet, sexy words while having sex.

How to do it right

- Begin with the both of you standing upright. You should both be facing the same direction.

- Then, grab your man's penis and insert it into either your butt or pussy from behind.

- Meet his thrusts by pushing your body back onto his.

Bendover Position:

Why your man will love it

This is another rear-entry standing position that's perfect for quickies. Much like the doggie style, this is another primal position that will allow him to reach in front and grab any part of your body that he pleases. Or if you'll allow it, he can grab your hair and bring out his inner caveman.

Why you'll love it too

The Bendover is a great deal less intimate than the Bodyguard position. That said, it's not such a bad idea to bring out your wild side from time to time. While making love, you can guide his hands to your front so he can fondle your boobs or play with your clit.

How to do it right

- Basically, all you need to do is to assume the Bodyguard position first.

- Then, once his cock is in you, simply lean over while stretching your arms out. Do this until your hands are able to come in contact with the floor.

- While your hubby is thrusting in and out of you, you may choose to meet his trusts by pushing back up against him or to just let him take control.

- Balance yourself with your arms and with your hands close to your feet.

Best Sex Positions for Her (have your husband/boyfriend read this section-as it is for them!)

Spooning Position:

Why your woman will love it

For most women, sex is all about the romance and the intimacy. The spooning position provides your woman with a feeling of safety. This position also makes her pussy tighter so she'll feel that you're bigger. Your woman will get more stimulation in the vaginal wall. It's also a great position for slow sex during lazy afternoons.

Why you'll love it too

Apart from the tighter fit, this is the perfect remedy for morning wood! Wake up in the morning, roll over towards your woman's side of the bed, and make a connection. Sure, this position is not meant for deep penetration but it will allow you to reach into the front and stroke her bits. You can also whisper naughty words to your mate.

How to do it right

- While facing the same way, both you and your woman should lie on your sides.

- Position yourself behind her and enter her gently from behind. You're woman's gonna have to bring her top leg slightly forward to ease your entry. Likewise, you'll need to lean over a little.

- Wrap your arms around your woman and fondle her tits for added intimacy.

- If you want to add more power to your thrusts, grab the top side of your woman's waist.

Butterfly Position:

Why your woman will love it

With this position, your penis will come directly in contact with her upper vaginal walls. This means your woman will get major G-spot stimulation leading to multiple orgasms. More than that, this position promotes intimacy through eye contact. It's also a good position for verbal and non-verbal communication during intercourse.

Why you'll love it too

Apart from the fact that you'll be giving your woman multiple O's, this modified missionary position places you in a power position, allowing you to control the pace of lovemaking.

How to do it right:

- Ask your woman to lie on her back. Her hips should be positioned close to the edge of your bed.

- Assume a standing position at the foot of the bed. Then, lift her hips upwards.

- Allow your woman to rest her thighs on your chest. Meanwhile, lay her calves on either side of your shoulders. Alternatively, you can have her legs wrapped around your waist.

- If you want to make your thrusts more vigorous, grab her thighs.

Criss Cross Position:

Why your woman will love it

The Criss Cross provides women with maximum clitoral stimulation.

Why you'll love it too

This position creates a tighter feel. Even when you're not on top, it's still a dominant position where you're able to control the thrusts. More than that, it allows deeper, more powerful strokes.

How to do it right:

- This position can be done on the bed or a on a table.

- Have your woman lie down on her back. Then, lift her legs so that they are pointing skyward.

- Then, stand up straight and penetrate her. While doing so, your woman should make sure that her legs are straight.

- Help her cross her legs at her ankles. After doing this, you'll immediately feel the tighter fit. The more she crosses her legs, the tighter her pussy will feel.

- Alternate your thrusts from deep and hard to quick and shallow.

Lotus Position:

Why your woman will love it

The Lotus is the most intimate sexual position ever invented, dating back from ancient times. In tantra, this is known as a sacred sex position that enables man and woman to connect not just physically but also emotionally and spiritually while having intercourse. This position requires you to look at each other face to face so you can maintain eye contact during sex or engage in deep and passionate kisses.

Why you'll love it too

Apart from the fact that you'll feel closer to your significant other, this provides your woman easy access to your back. She can provide you with an erotic back rub while making love to you. This is also a good position if you enjoy having your ears and your neck licked.

How to do it right

- Assume a cross-legged sitting position on bed. You may also choose to do this on the floor or on any flat surface. Just imagine that you're about to do yoga.

- Then, ask your woman to lower herself onto you while facing you.

- Her arms and her legs should end up wrapped around your body.

- Do the same thing and envelop her in your arms.

- Your woman will then make back and forth rocking movements.

- As she does this, kiss your woman's neck and gaze into her face. Whisper some loving words to her. You can tell her how lovely she looks or how good it feels making love to her.

Pearly Gates Position:

Why your woman will love it

This is a position that will make your woman feel exposed. Nevertheless, she'll love it. She'll like the sense of abandon that this position will provide her with. Because it's somewhat similar to the spooning position, she'll also feel a sense of security and intimacy.

Why you'll love it too

This is a simple yet inventive position that's rarely done by couples in bed. Furthermore, it'll give you easy access to her front side if you want to masturbate her while entering her from behind.

How to do it right

- The two of you should lie on the bed while facing the same way.

- Make sure that your knees are bent and that your feet are flat on the bed.

- Ask your woman to lie on her back on top of you. It's just like spooning but the difference is you're both looking upward.

- Assist your woman in balancing herself. Put your arms around her waist or her chest. Ask her to spread out her arms and her legs.

- Put your cock into her butt or pussy. Then, keeping your feet flat on the bed, thrust into her. You can also reach in front of your woman to give her a hand, so to speak.

- Make this lovemaking position more intimate by kissing her neck and uttering words of affection into your woman's ear.

Chapter 3-Best Oral Sex Techniques for Women

We are going to talk about how to please your man as much as possible. There are very few things that turn your man on more than a blowjob.

First lets talk about a couple of obstacles you might face with blowjobs first:

Pubic hair:

A little bit of a bush above his cock isn't such a bad thing. However, in general most girls like well-groomed pubic hair or completely shaved pubic hair-as a hairy bush creates a barrier for oral sex. Hair in his butt and perineum are usually prevalent. A full Brazilian wax along with regular shaving can prevent this. If your man has a bush barrier, encourage him to continue to shave his pubes. Otherwise it will limit his ability to be pleased by you!

The unfresh penis:

After a long day of work, dinner, and putting the kids to bed…. It is understandable for your man to be hesitant to let your face near his penis and butt. As I always recommend- always shower before having sex. It leaves a nice fresh feeling down there.

Now that we've talked about a couple of obstacles, its time to give some more tips on giving oral to your man:

Surprise him at the door:

A quick unexpected blowjob when he least expects it when he walks through the door at home is sexy. About 34% of men wish that their woman would surprise them with oral sex as they walk through the door. When he walks through the door, kiss him, ask him how his day was, and then surprise him by ripping his cock out and giving him head.

Don't forget about his balls or perineum:

Don't neglect the balls. Playing with his balls is a must when it comes to oral, because they are often neglected during intercourse. Cradle his balls, suck each one in your mouth, nibble a little, and don't forget to stroke. While you are caressing the balls, go towards the shaft and go up and down with your tongue.

The perineum (the area between his penis/balls and his butt) are also often ignored too. This is an extremely sensitive area for both men and women. Nibble this area, kiss it up and down, and put pressure with your finger down there.

Spit on it!

A sexy thing to do before you give your man a blowjob is to spit on his cock. Massage his cock and rub the saliva all over the shaft and head of his penis. This makes his cock stickier and juicier. You can also do this to his balls, perineum and butthole as well.

Roleplay:

I have an upcoming book on naughty sex-but to summarize exploring different roleplaying is a huge turn on. Dressing up like a slutty secretary or a sexy teacher is an awesome foreplay method.

Tease him first:

Gradually build up. You don't want to be giving head to a limp penis. Instead, as I always say-incorporate some foreplay first. Several minutes of groping, hand playing and making out are a great way to start. You can also kiss and lick his inner thighs several inches from his penis. This area is very sensitive and is a huge turn on.

Here are some awesome blowjob positions:

The Regular blowjob position:

This is the standard blowjob position. Have your man lay on his back with his legs spread open. Lie on your stomach and place your head near his penis and give him head.

The Kneeling blowjob position:

This is a basic blowjob position as well. Essentially while your man is sitting down you kneel over and put his cock in your mouth. Try a variety of locations to see what works for you, as you could try it on a chair, couch, the floor, etc.

The Cinema blowjob position:

This is called the Cinema blowjob position because it can be performed while seeing a movie at a theater (if you feel like being really naughty.....). Simply sit next to your man (either to the right or left), bend over where your head is looking down on his cock, and give head. You don't have to do this in a movie theater though. You can simply surprise him when you and your man are watching a movie by pulling his cock out of his pants (without his permission) and giving head.

Southern exposure position:

This is when your man lies on the bed on his back, lifts his feet and legs in the air and spreads his legs open-exposing his penis, balls, and butthole. This gives you the opportunity to devour all his erogenous zones, including his perineum and butthole. It should also be mentioned that having a man's butthole licked can drive him crazy.

The 69:

Most people know this one, but this might be the best position. While your man is lying on his back- "sit on his face" so your pussy is on his mouth, and then bend over until you can reach and place his cock in your mouth. Blow him while he eats you out!

The 69 on your sides:

This is basically the 69 except where you and your man both rotate where you both are on your side.

Fuck Face Sex Position

The name says it all—he fucks you on the face while kneeling over your chest. While it may sound too brazen for some women, it actually makes your man feel hot and special because of the special treatment-treating him like a porn star to be exact. Allowing him to hump while in your mouth does not work well if you have a shallow gagging reflex, but you can expect him to appreciate your efforts more if you allow him to take some control and let you swallow some juice at the end.

The Face Plow:

This is similar to the Fuck face position-except this is a male dominant position. You will be lying on your back while you man places his knees a few inches away from both sides of your head. His penis and balls should be hanging over your nose and mouth. He will then place the head of his cock into your mouth and start thrusting. This position is great for when you are in the mood for being submissive to your man-as he is clearly in control.

Now that we've talked about a few blowjob positions-lets talk abut swallowing. After you perform a number of these positions-your man is surely going to be horny and will cum all over the place. You are probably going to be tempted to swallow his load and let him cum inside your mouth. Here are some things to note on swallowing:

Only swallow if he is completely STI free!

With an intense sex life it is recommended to get checked in by an STI clinic regularly. If your man is completely STI free-swallowing his cum is harmless. It is dangerous to your health to swallow unhealthy cum.

Make sure he eats healthy beforehand:

Cum naturally tastes bitter and salty (according to research.... I'm not speaking from experience here!). Assuming your man is completely STI free and you are safe to swallow-make sure he eats healthy beforehand. If your man has healthy eating habits during the day-his cum is likely going to taste better and be easier to swallow. However-if he eats anything unhealthy or greasy-then his cum will likely taste nasty and will be a hard swallow.

Deepthroat if you have trouble swallowing:

If you love the act of swallowing but do not like the taste of cum-then make sure that you give deepthroating a try. Make sure you put the head of his cock as deep into your mouth as you can so you can swallow while minimizing the taste.

Use a mint:

This is another tip for those who do not like the taste of cum. The mint leaves your mouth very fresh and can help kill the taste of semen if you don't like it. Pop some mints in your mouth before the blowjob.

Chapter 4-How to give him a rim job

If you don't know what a rim job/rimming or analingus are-it is the art of sucking, caressing, and licking your partner's butthole. For obvious reasons-this can be gross if done wrong. However, if done properly this can be extremely sexy, as it is easy to have a peak experience when your butthole is being attacked. The butthole is a sensitive area!

Rimming is not for everyone. But to many watching a clean and fit man having his asshole licked is a hot and steamy thing. Imagine a hot, wet, naked male celebrity such as Ryan Gosling walking out of the shower. You'd want to lick every inch of him, including all over his butt!

The butthole has a ton of nerve endings, which is why analingus can be so sexy. Men will be surprised with how much they like it if they have never tried it before. So give it a try!

Here are some tips on rimming:

Shower first!

The first tip with analingus is to make sure you and your partner have both showered beforehand (as you always should before sex). The reason is obvious-as the anus is the area of most concern regarding hygiene. However-as long as you and your partner have showered and have washed each others' genitals well analingus should be fun.

Foreplay is a must!

Just walking up to your man and immediately sucking and licking on his butthole won't work for peak experience. Shoving your tongue up his ass is only half the battle.

Communicate through dirty talk or intimacy beforehand to build up the anticipation.

On his back, legs spread open:

This is one way you can perform analingus. While your naked man is lying on his back with his legs spread wide open is a great opportunity to blow him. Play, caress, and lick his penis and balls first. This alone should turn him on. Then, while sucking and licking his cock or balls take one or two of your fingers and gently move them in circles on and around his butthole. This will build up anticipation. Kiss, nibble, and lick his perineum (the area between his butt and penis). Finally, surprise him by lifting his buttcheeks up and giving him an aggressive tongue attack up his butthole. Switching between aggressively licking his butthole and slowly/passionately licking and kissing his butthole will drive him absolutely crazy. While you are performing analingus, massage his penis and balls.

Face down, ass up:

This is the second major method on where analingus is performed, where your man is on his hands and knees with his legs spread out so his penis, balls, and butt are in your face. His penis and balls are parallel to his legs and pointing to the ground. Since his cock is likely going to be hard-do not bend it backwards, as this will hurt! So you have to lick his penis and balls from behind. Begin by licking the shaft of his cock from behind and gently nibbling his balls. Play and caress with his balls and his cock. Then, you can alternate from licking his shaft to kissing his buttcheeks and then slowly making it to kissing his butthole. Once you start moving your mouth towards his butthole, make sure you continue to play with his penis and balls. Be sure to kiss and nibble on the perineum as well. Finally, start licking and sucking on his butthole and cheeks. Spitting on his butthole and using your fingers to rub the saliva around his butthole and perineum are a great sexy addition to this.

Sex Games:

35 Naughty Sex Games to make your Sex Life Hot!

Introduction

Are you looking to bring your sex up a notch? Do you have a more naughty, kinky side to you?

Then this book is for you! Throughout this book you will learn naughty oral sex tips, rough sex tips, and some sex games all to spice up your sex life! Sex is exciting and should always be exciting. This book shows you how to always do that.

Here is a synopsis of what you will learn:

-What Naughty Sex Is

-Naughty Oral Sex Tips for Him

-Naughty Oral Sex Tips for Her

-Rough Sex Tips

-35 Sex Games

Chapter 1 – Naughty Sex Basic Tips

Don't get caught up in vanilla sex! You are on a quest for a more exciting, sexy, and kinky sex life. Don't apologize for wanting to make things a little more naughty in your relationship. Here are some basics ideas to make your sex life more naughty:

Being submissive:

Both men and women fantasize about this. It is dead sexy to have your partner completely in control and completely have their way with you!

Being dominant:

This is the complete opposite of being submissive. You know you love the idea of tying your partner down and doing whatever you want with them!

Group sex:

Everyone fantasizes about this. Men love to fantasize about a threesome with their wife/girlfriend along with a hot Asian or Latina woman involved. There's nothing sexier than having anal sex with your wife/girlfriend while watching her eat out another woman's pussy!

Women typically fantasized being worshipped by her partner and another man. One man can penetrate her while the other receives a blowjob from her.

A great way to make this fantasy a reality is to join a local swinger club. Couples are encouraged to live out their fantasies there!

Exhibitionism:

Some sort of public sex-whether it be filming a porno between you and your partner-or fucking in a public place are fantasies all men and women are likely to have at some point in their lives.

Filming a porno is not recommended for obvious reasons. While it is legal it can have serious professional consequences if your friends/families/coworkers find out! Having sex in a public area is a much more commonly fulfilled fantasy. However-use with caution and make sure you don't get caught, as this can have serious legal consequences!

Strap on sex:

This is a fantasy held by women where they play the "man" for the night and wear a "strap-on" penis. Both the woman and even the man have fun with this-as the woman will enjoy being the aggressor for the night and penetrating the man. Having her man vulnerable to this kind of sex is an incredible turn-on for women. You can purchase a strap-on penis at a local adult store.

Juicy Sex:

Both sexes fantasize about their partner releasing all their juices all over their faces/bodies. Have sex to the point where either the woman squirts all over the man or the man cums all over the woman's body.

Chapter 2 – Naughty Oral Sex Tips for Her:

If you are a man reading this book-have your wife or girlfriend read this section. This chapter reveals some naughty tips for her to devour you down there!

Invisible Oral:

Turn the lights out while you devour his cock. This element of surprise is exciting to him because he doesn't know what you will do to him. The lack of sight also enhances his sensations down there.

Gagging:

Take his cock and suck on it. Bring it as far into your throat as you can so that you are not choking on it but just enough to make you gag. This will drive him crazy.

Ambush him at the door:

A quick unexpected blowjob when he least expects it when he walks through the door at home is sexy. About 34% of men wish that their woman would surprise them with oral sex as they walk through the door. When he walks through the door, kiss him, ask him how his day was, and then surprise him by ripping his cock out and giving him head.

Spit on it!

A sexy thing to do before you give your man a blowjob is to spit on his cock. Massage his cock and rub the saliva all over the shaft and head of his penis. This makes his cock stickier and juicier. You can also do this to his balls, perineum and butthole as well.

Play with his balls and pressure his perineum:

Don't neglect the balls. Playing with his balls is a must when it comes to oral, because they are often neglected during intercourse. Cradle his balls, suck each one in your mouth, nibble a little, and don't forget to stroke. While you are caressing the balls, go towards the shaft and go up and down with your tongue.

The perineum (the area between his penis/balls and his butt) is also often ignored too. This is an extremely sensitive area for both men and women. Nibble this area, kiss it up and down, and put pressure with your finger down there.

Lick the tip of his cock:

The meatus-which is the hole that is the tip of his penis-is an extremely sensitive area. Licking and applying pressure with your tongue there is a huge turn on.

Be enthusiastic and horny:

Many guys are worried that their wife/girlfriend do not like giving head. Show him you love it! Suck his cock aggressively and smile while you do it. Bonus if you can make seductive eye contact with him while you are at it.

The Breast Stroke:

Lie on your back and have your man place his penis between your boobs. Have him thrust towards your face. Tilt your head towards your boobs and open your mouth and catch his cock inside your mouth every time he makes a thrust.

Attack multiple areas:

If you want your man to cum more easily, make sure your mouth and hands are both always busy. When you are sucking on his penis, play with his balls and massage his perineum. When you are licking and kissing his butt, massage his cock and his balls. Double or triple the sensation for him and he will cum all over the place.

A Hot Spot:

A hot spot women often miss is a patch of skin on his penis that is right between his cock's base and testicles. Gently nibbling and sucking on that area will make him lose his mind.

Rim Jobs:

If you don't know what a rim job is-it is the art of sucking, licking, and kissing your partner's butthole. Rim jobs, if done right, can be seriously hot. Make sure your man has showered previously (for obvious reasons.....). Have your man take the "face down, ass up," position. Lick and suck the back of his cock, and then slowly lick the shaft of his cock upwards toward his balls. Continue to massage his cock while you now kiss and lick his balls. Gently nibble on both of his balls while moving upward to his perineum. Gently nibble and lick on his perineum while you continue to massage his cock and balls. Finally, kiss the area around his butthole, and then devour his butthole with your tongue. You can also spit on his butthole and rub the saliva from his butthole down to his balls and cock. This will all surely drive him crazy.

Chapter 3 – Naughty Oral Sex Tips for Him:

If you are a woman reading this book-have your husband or boyfriend read this section. This chapter reveals some naughty tips for her to devour you down there!

Use your hands:

Grab her buttcheeks while you are driving your tongue into her pussylips. This intensifies the feeling. Giving oral without using your hands properly is just awkward. You can also finger fuck her from the bottom of her pussy while licking her at the same time.

For maximum orgasm it is important to always use your hands. When you are eating her pussy, make sure you are either fingering her or squeezing her buttcheeks. When you are licking and kissing her butt, continue to massage or finger her pussy.

Spit on it!

A sexy thing to do before you give your woman oral is to spit on her pussy. Massage her pussy and rub the saliva all over the lips of her vagina. This makes her pussy juicier. You can also do this to her perineum and butthole as well.

Switch between aggressive and passive oral sex:

Start out slow. Gradually kiss her inner thighs, her perineum, and gently rub her clitoris with one finger. Then slowly move towards kissing her pussylips. Afterwards, slowly enter 1 finger into her pussy. Then move to two fingers or more. The key though is to move slowly.

Afterwards, aggressively give her pussy or butt a tongue attack. Women love a man who can consistently switch between slowly and deeply giving her love and aggressively giving her love.

Food Sex:

Why eat your dinner off of platters and silverware when you can eat off of each other's naked bodies? Give this a try every now and then. Good foods to incorporate with sex are: chocolate, strawberries, bananas, whipped cream, cherries, melons, ice cream, bacon, and champagne. Lick any of these off of your woman's parts.

Have her sit on your face:

This is incredibly sexy because it shows how close your partner is willing to get with you. Have her "sit on your face" and eat away! Have her move her hips up and down so she is giving you a face-rub with her pussy and butt.

Rim Jobs:

If you don't know what a rim job is-it is the art of sucking, licking, and kissing your partner's butthole. Rim jobs, if done right, can be seriously hot. Make sure your woman has showered previously (for obvious reasons.....). Have her sit in the "face down, ass up" position. Begin by devouring her pussy. Make sure to finger her vagina while licking away. Slowly begin nibbling and licking on her perineum (the area between her butt and pussy)." Continue to finger her clit during this time. Finally, kiss the area around her butthole, and then devour her butthole with your tongue. You can also spit on her butthole and rub the saliva from her butthole down to her perineum and pussy. This will all surely make her scream!

Chapter 4 – Rough Sex 101:

Don't stick to basic vanilla sex. Change it up! Rough sex does not need to be that "rough" but it is a great way to add kinks to your sex life.

However, make sure that both you and your partner consent. You don't want to be pulling your partner's hair or spanking your partner without their consent.

Here are the best rough sex tips:

Know your fantasies beforehand: Both men and women have their kinks and fetishes. Make sure that you and your partner discuss with each others fantasies first. If one of you has a particular fetish that the other one finds appalling, its important to know in advance.

Scream and yell: This intensifies the feeling and environment of your sex session. Make sure no one else can hear you though!

Nibble and bite (gently): This is great for erogenous zones such as the vagina, balls, penis, boobs, perineum, the butthole, the neck, belly, and inner thighs.

Claw your lover (again, gently).

Aggressive movements. Pounding and fucking each other aggressively like there's no tomorrow will turn you two on like nothing else.

Pulling each other's hair. Pulling your woman's hair while you are fucking her up her ass is dead sexy.

Slapping each other. A light slap across the face or your partner's butt is great for this.

Abusive dirty talk. Read my books on talking dirty for more about this! But saying to each other "fuck me like you hate me" or "call me a bitch!" are huge turn-ons.

Anal Sex: Although anal sex can be moderately painful for women, it is still hot. More women are wanting to give anal sex a try. Don't thrust too hard though!

Forcing your partner to perform sexual acts. For example, shoving your cock down your woman's throat is great for this. Sitting on your man's face and pressuring him to devour your pussy is extremely hot.

Spanking. Aggressive spanking, although can be moderately painful, can add some extra spice to your sex. It makes your woman feel like a pornstar. Ask her if she likes it when you slap her ass.

Light Choking: Grasping your hand over your lover's neck and gripping firmly (but not choking) is a fetish for many people because it reduces the flow of oxygen to the brain, creating a sort of dizziness.

Whipping: You can get a bdsm whip from a sex store. This goes in hand with submission. Show her she is misbehaving by whipping her!

Dominance and submission: Both men and women fantasize about either dominating their partner or being dominated by their partner. This is because it is extremely hot knowing that your partner can do whatever they want with you..... and you have no control over it!

Sex toys and gags.

Chapter 5 – Naughty places to have sex

Think about all the wildest and craziest places that you fantasized about having sex. Make it a reality! Relationship expert Emily Morse, Ph. D., says that expanding your sexual experiences outside of the bedroom leads to more spontaneity and more closeness with your partner. Great sex experiences are great for conversation with your partner and are great for making good memories with your partner.

Getting it on in different places is more about the new and exciting experiences you will have with your partner and not just about orgasm or ejaculation. By having new sex experiences in different places-you will learn more about yourself and what turns you and your partner on.

Many of the below locations are public-so use with caution!

Awesome place to have sex with your partner:

Your backyard: having sex in the backyard is a great place to get it on when you don't want to have to worry about getting caught but still want to do it outside.

The couch: fucking your woman on the couch with multiple pillows under your woman's back can increase the likelihood of orgasm.

Hotel Sex: A hotel has all the benefits of sex with none of the normal responsibilities of being an adult. You don't have to worry about making the bed or clean up-as housekeeping takes care of that. Plus-if you ever want to have crazy loud sex so that your kids won't hear-a hotel is a great place to go for an offsite fuckfest!

A public event: Weddings, sports events, parties, etc. This adds to the thrill of "we just might get caught." Definitely do this one when you want that excitement to be really high. Find a bathroom or a closet farthest away from the crowd.

If you only have a few minutes, this is a great opportunities to give her a quickie through her skirt-as this is easy to cover up if someone is coming!

Mirror Sex: Sex in front of the mirror is a huge turn on for women because she can see how she looks while jumping your bones.

On the Beach: This inherently is one of the most romantic places to have sex. However, make sure to do it on a towel-as you don't want sand getting in your vagina or butthole.

An Empty College Classroom or Library: This is a naughty one. Check the class or library hours to make sure you won't get interrupted. It is recommended that she wears a skirt or dress with no panties just to make the "in and out" easier.

A Park: Look for a beautiful park to do this on. Bring a tent or blanket with you!

An elevator: This one is naughty too and the risk of getting caught is high. However, its extremely hot. I would recommend saving this one for buildings or locations that aren't that busy. Make sure there isn't a security camera in the elevator!

A closet: Whether it be a party, event, or even at a friends house-fucking in a closet is hot.

A Jacuzzi: Book a room with a Jacuzzi if you don't own one. This too is one of the more romantic locations to get it on.

A limousine: This is great if you are having a limousine transport you somewhere and you can't keep your hands off each other during the ride. Make sure that the privacy window is down though.... Don't distract the driver!

A waterbed: This is a step up from regular sex in the bed. The slip and slide makes things rougher and more fun.

Private office party: If you have keys to a private office- show your partner how hard you work on that desk (in a different way).

A boat: Getting it on with waves in the background is awesome.

On a roof: This is still outside yet still gives you some privacy. However-don't be too loud!

The woods: It is beautiful to have sex where there is nothing but nature all around you. However, this is exciting and thrilling-because you never know if someone will walk by!

Chapter 6 – 35 Naughty Sex Games

Here are some more steamy games you and your partner can play!

Sex Game 1-The time bomb: For this game-set a time limit (10 minutes, 20 minutes, etc.) where you focus just on foreplay (i.e. kissing, touching, groping, teasing, etc.) for that period of time. However, no penetration or oral is allowed during this time

This game is great because it allows you to have a "pregame" before a wild sex session. Foreplay is critical!

Sex Game 2-Blind sex: Take a blindfold and keep on your partner for a period of time. This is hot for sex because this causes certain senses to be enhanced due to the lack of sight.

Sex Game 3-Prisoner sex: Tie up your partner (assuming he or she consents) to a position where they are submissive to you. You can use ties, ropes, or materials you can get from sex stores. Tie your partner up and do whatever you want with them!

Sex Game 4-Twister: Find a parking lot where no one else is. Have sex in the car in that parking lot. Make believe that your partner is a virgin. Give them step by step instructions on how to give you oral and how to have sex with you. This one is fun because it is a blast from the past, and also because it gives the two of you the opportunity to try new things!

Sex Game 5-Kinky Cards: Play cards and give each suit a sexual meaning, act, or position. Use a timer for, say, five minutes. When someone picks a particular suit, they either perform or receive that sexual act for five minutes.

Sex Game 6-Truth or Dare: Use this game as a way to find out more about your partner's sex fantasies and be more raunchy!

Sex Game 7-This is war: Get naked with your partner and have a pillow fight. Whoever surrenders first has to be submissive and do whatever sexual act the winner wants.

Sex Game 8- Fantasy Bowl: Each of you put your top ten sex fantasies on a small piece of paper and put them in a fishbowl. Talk about them together, why you think they are hot, and make them happen!

Sex Game 9-Role Playing: The man can pretend to be a doctor, and the woman can pretend to be the patient. The doctor can pretend he's examining the woman and use excuses to touch her in her erogenous zones. There are endless options for roleplaying. Use your imagination!

Sex Game 10-Would you rather?: Ask your partner dirty "would you rather" questions. This will get kinky and raunchy quick!

Sex Game 11-Strip Questions: Ask your partner some personal questions. If they get it wrong, have them remove an item of clothing and chug a shot of alcohol.

Sex Game 12-Sexy Dice: Assign a sex position to each dice. Once you role the dice and it lands on a certain number, perform the proper sex act on your partner.

Sex Game 13-Tarzan and Jane: Start out with the two of you in bed. The guy attempts to wrestle the girl, tie his girl's hands to the bed rest so he can penetrate her. The girl tries to resist. This game can be really fun. After a few minutes though, both the man and the woman will become really horny and it will lead to rough sex.

Sex Game 14-Blindfolds and food sex: This game requires ice cream. Blindfold your partner and give your partner a spoon. Have your partner attempt to feed you. If any of the ice cream drips on your body, they have to eat it off. In time they will be eating off in many places!

Sex Game 15-Reenact a porn scene: Watch a really horny kinky sex scene with your partner. Reenact every sex act exactly as in the scene.

Sex Game 16-Strip Pong: Play normal beer pong. Except once one of you scores, the other has to remove an item of clothing each time. The first one entirely naked loses, and has to give a sexual favor of the winner's choice.

Sex Game 17-One Step forward, One Step back: The woman lies naked in bed while the man stands at the door. He desperately wants to penetrate his partner. The woman asks him a question about her. If he gets it right, he gets a step forward. If he gets it wrong, he has to step back. He persists in this game until he makes it to the bed and gets some pussy!

Sex Game 18-Sports: While watching a sports game, you and your partner choose competing teams. When one team scores, the partner with the winning team gets to receive any sex favor from the other partner for five minutes.

Sex Game 19-Seven Minutes in Heaven: This is where the man locks himself and his woman in a small closet. He gets to do whatever he wants to sexually to his woman.

Sex Game 20-Sex toy hide-and-seek: hide sex toys around the house and have your partner find them. Once your partner finds one, they have to use it on you.

Sex Game 21-20 Kinky Questions: Have your partner ask you 20 questions to guess what your favorite sex fantasy is.

Ask questions like "Does it involve toys?" "Does it involve more than two people?"

Sex Game 22-Marco Polo: Next time the two of you are swimming in a pool alone-play Marco Polo. Once you two find each other-pull each others bathing suit bottoms off and get it on right there.

Sex Game 23-Orgasm rotation: Lie naked next to each other and play with each others' penis and vagina. Whomever comes first gives the other person oral sucking until the other comes. Repeat.

Sex Game 24-"Don't get caught" masturbation: Grope each other sexually in a public place such as a restaurant when no one else is watching. This adds to the arousal because you know that you might just get caught!

Sex Game 25- Mirror each other: Sit naked right in front of each other and starting kissing and licking each other. When one partner kisses or licks part of their partner, the other partner "mirrors" their actions and kisses and licks their partner in the same area.

Sex Game 26-Blindfold games: blindfold your naked man or woman. Then pour some chocolate sauce on your naked body. Your man or woman has to lean over and kiss and lick your body until he or she finds the chocolate with his or her tongue. Once they lick all the chocolate off of your body-rotate roles! It's your turn to put the blindfold on.

Sex Game 27-The "Try Not to Have Sex" Game: This game is good for building up sexual lust and sounds counterintuitive. You and your partner are both naked and continue to make out with each other. However, you both try to avoid having sex with each other. This avoidance ironically builds sexual tension. Once one of you gives in and attempts sex with the other-that person loses.

Sex Game 28-Slippery Steamy Sex-This is great when you and your partner either get out of a sauna or steam room. You and your partner will both have steamy bodies. This will make sex even hotter.

Sex game 29- Food oral: Take a scoop of ice cream and put it in your mouth. Then, give head to your man or lick your woman's pussy with the ice cream in your mouth. Warn your partner first-as it will give them a cold shock!

Sex Game 30- 30 seconds of pleasure: This encourages fast and aggressive sex. Have a timer for 30 seconds and let your partner do whatever they want to with you for 30 seconds. Once the 30 seconds is up-switch roles!

Sex Game 31-Spin the bottle: Spin the bottle, but instead of kissing-if the bottle points at you-you get to perform a sexual act on your partner of your choosing.

Sex Game 32-Sexy scavenger hunt: Make a list of all the sexy things your partner has to do and hide them around the house. Once he or she finds them-they perform the act on you.

Sex Game 33-Sex Monopoly: While playing a game of monopoly-instead of buying properties, "buy" pieces of your partner's clothes.

Sex Game 34-Body shots: This involves both of you being naked and using a dice, paper, and alcohol. Make a list of erogenous zones (boobs, pussy, perineum, etc.) and number them 1-6 on a piece of paper. When you role the dice, your pour the body shot on that area and lick/suck the alcohol off.

Sex Game 35-Be strangers: Agree to meet your partner at a bar, but pretend not to know each other. Make believe you are meeting for the first time, and engage in small talk. Once you "get to know" them, ask them over to your place and have the best make believe one-night stand of your life.

Spice Up Your Sex Life!

How to be maintain an awesome sex life with your partner and live your wildest sexual fantasies!

Introduction

Are you looking to take your relationship to the next level?

Many couples date, get married, go on a honeymoon, all living through this intense firey passion for each other. Yet, as the years go by couples can get bogged down by the monotony of the "real world" and can lose the excitement in the physical and intimate relationship with their partner that they once had.

This book will help you understand why and how to maintain a strong sex life. It specifically addresses many of the sex fantasies and adventures you can explore to take your relationship to the next level instead of going through the "same old, same old."

Here is a synopsis of what you will learn:

-Common killers of sex drive

-Why a strong sex life is important to the foundation of your relationship

-The most common sexual fantasies between men and women

-Best places to have sex

Chapter 1 – Why Sex Dies Down

Everybody loves sex-but why do people always joke that "Marriage is the end of sex?" It has been estimated that at least 40 million Americans are having a "sexless marriage"- as in having sex no more than ten times a year.

A continuous sex life is important for your health and can satisfy all sorts of physical and emotional needs. Yet why do people stop doing it? Below are some of the top reasons:

You're too busy

It's easy to get stuck in the daily routine where you wake up, take a shower, work your 9-to-5, drive home, cook dinner, put the kids to bed, and hit the sack. Rinse and repeat. However, if you let the "daily grind" get to you for too long and take priority over sex-your relationship is headed for trouble.

Don't let the everyday grind get to you. Sex is a great way for you and your partner to "get out of your head". Find a way to make it work. Delegate more tasks to your children, hire someone to take care of some of the daily monotonous tasks......whatever. Do what you need to do to make time for regular sex!

Your bedroom doesn't set the tone for sex

You and your partner's bedroom should be used for two things..... sleep and sex. That's it! Get rid of the unnecessary technology and distractions. Keep tech, newspapers, out of your bedroom and make it a tech free zone. It's hard to be in the mood for sex when your partner is stuck on his or her iPhone.

You always put the kids priorities first

Often times couples have a hard time saying no to their kids. They spend too much time taking care of their kids needs first. Throughout the process-they often become so busy with the kids that they forget who they were as a couple.

Frank Grillo (famous actor) was interviewed on the Huffington Post. He said his secret to a happy marriage was "Never Put the Kids First." Always love and take care of your kids but make a decision with your partner that in order to be the best parent you can be-you need to put your relationship with your partner.

Always putting the kids first, letting the kids sleep in bed with you-can be a recipe for disaster for your sex life. Be clear with your partner that the only way you can be a good parent is to be a good team-and in order to do that you have to put yourselves and your relationship first. Sex is a priority for you and your partner. Never forget that.

You have boring, routine sex.

To repeat what was stated above-it is easy to let the daily life turn into a monotonous routine. When you do have sex you do the "same old, same old" positions, moves, and locations. Don't get stuck in a rut. Spontaneity and being unpredictable are key to excitement in any relationship.

I highlight sex adventures in chapters 3, 4, and 5. Hang on to get out of the rut!

You don't take care of yourself. Would you have sex with you?

Often times after couples get married-they let themselves go! Couples will often gain some weight, stop taking care of their hygiene, stop shaving their pubes.......etc. You need to take care of yourself if you want your relationship to thrive-you've got to take care of yourself! Being married and getting used to each other is no excuse to sell yourself short.

Keep wearing perfume/cologne like you used to. Wear slutty lingerie like you used to. Get naked with your partner more often. Don't wait for your partner to tell you that you need to take care of yourself-because they probably won't.

Failure to address sexual dysfunction

Men will likely suffer from erectile difficulties, and women will likely have difficulty achieving orgasms. Embarrassment about these issues often causes people to avoid having sex with their partner to avoid the humiliation.

There are good solutions that can address these problems. Men with erectile dysfunction can benefit from erectile disorder medications such as Cialis, Viagra, or Levitra. This restores confidence, and also makes sex relatively worry free.

For women, difficulties in orgasm can because by issues of anxiety, or simply issues of sexual technique. Sex therapy can be very helpful to address these problems.

The key point here is to accept that you will likely face sexual dysfunction at some point and need to be willing to take the proper steps to fix it and not be afraid to talk to your partner about the ordeal.

You don't have any anticipation or foreplay to sex

Many couples are unaware that foreplay to sex actually begins first thing in the morning. Showing kindness, affection, respect, admiration — are all forms of foreplay. Giving compliments telling your partner that they are looking sexy or handsome can lead to anticipation. Simple intimacy can get them in the mood as well. Physical intimacy-such as a kiss in passing, or a slapping of your partner's butt can cause arousal and lead to anticipation. Caressing and sexual touch should be a part of your daily life outside the bedroom. The importance of touch and intimacy cannot be overstated.

Simple sexy text messages sent throughout the day can lead to anticipation as well (aka "sexting"). Simply texting a romantic gesture can excite your partner and get them excited to see you at the end of the day. You can feel free to check out my other books on "Dirty Talk" and "Sexting" for more information about this!

Chapter 2 – Why you should embrace your sex lives, keep having sex, and keep exploring new sex adventures

Sex is awesome and we all know it. Embrace that and that sex is a cornerstone to a strong relationship. The more intimate and physical your relationship is the better.

Here are some more reasons that you should always maintain strong sex drive and be looking to improve your sex life:

Sex is unique between you and your spouse.

Among the many ideal characteristics of marriage is that it enables couples to share sexual intimacy with each other and only with each other. The fact that the two of you are married makes sex more valuable because it becomes a pleasurable experience that you can uniquely and exclusively share with your spouse and not with anyone else. Without sex, your husband/wife is literally reduced to the role of a roommate. Thus, the fact that sex is essential to a successful marriage is certainly an understatement.

Sex makes married life a whole lot easier.

When married couples allow sex life to jump out of the window, this creates a massive strain in the relationship. This may not always be obvious but little by little, the effects manifest themselves through lack of patience, irritability, insecurities, doubt, and subconscious resentment. On the other hand, married couples who have active sex lives tend to be more relaxed. They become happier, more tolerant, and more open-minded. Simply put, sex in marriage helps in smoothing over the trials that married couples inevitably encounter on a daily basis. You'll be surprised to find out how, after solving the sexual issues in your marriage, everything else will eventually fall into place.

The typical situation in problematic marriages goes like this:

The husband wants to have more sex while the wife doesn't. For the husband, sex is what enables him to feel close to his wife. The wife cannot understand why he needs sex in order to feel close. She doesn't see why he can't achieve a sense of closeness through talking, cuddling, and just spending time with her. Meanwhile, the husband cannot understand why sexual intercourse does not make his wife feel close to him. Then, the wife begins wondering why sex is so important to her husband. She begins wondering whether there's something wrong with her.

The reason for this is because men and women are wired differently. While women associate romance with emotions, men's perception of romance is strongly associated with sexual affirmation. For men, sex is a verification of their vitality. Sex, especially certain forms of sex such as oral sex, affirm his manhood and makes him feel that you love, respect, and honor all of him.

Here's another typical real life scenario:

The wife worries why her husband lacks interest in her. She does her best to be attractive from spending long hours at the gym to walking around the house in lingerie that are too slutty for her tastes. Yet, the most response she gets from him is a reminder to iron his shirt in the morning. She begins to worry why her husband no longer finds her sexy. This realization damages her self-esteem. She starts feeling embarrassed for having to constantly seduce him. She begins to worry that he's seeing someone else or that she's just not as hot as younger women. Soon, she develops resentment towards her husband.

In both cases, the ultimate effect is emotional detachment between the couples.

What men fail to understand is that their sexual advances make their wives feel special. She needs constant reassurance that you love her and that you still find her attractive after all these years. In other words, your sexual advances affirm her value. All in all, whether you're a man or a woman, you like to feel wanted and needed in your marriage

Sex Reduces Stress.

Sex will relax and reduce your stress levels! During sex-our bodies produce dopamine, endorphins and oxytocin-all which increase our levels of happiness and enhances desire.

Sex Makes You Look Younger.

According to science-having sex at least three times a week can apparently make you appear 10 years younger! Why worry about anti aging treatments when you can simply have more sex!

Dr. David Weeks, a former head of old age psychology at the Royal Edinburgh Hospital, spent 10 years surveying thousands of men and women of different age ranges. All respondents between the ages of 40 and 50 who looked younger had sex at least three times per week. Pleasure from sex is a critical factor in maintaining your youth.

Sex reminds you of who you are as a couple

This is why increasing the frequency and the quality of sex in your marriage is so important. Sex with your spouse reminds you what brought you together in the first place. This doesn't just pertain to the physical attraction but also to the emotional and mental connection that made you want to spend the rest of your life with that person. Sex with your husband/wife will remind you that you're more than just a mom/dad but vital sexual beings with needs and desires.

Chapter 3 – Common Sexual Fantasies Couples have

Being submissive:

Both men and women fantasize about this. It is dead sexy to have your partner completely in control and completely have their way with you!

Being dominant:

This is the complete opposite of being submissive. You know you love the idea of tying your partner down and doing whatever you want with them!

Group sex:

Everyone fantasizes about this. Men love to fantasize about a threesome with their wife/girlfriend along with a hot Asian or Latina woman involved. There's nothing sexier than having anal sex with your wife/girlfriend while watching her eat out another woman's pussy!

Women typically fantasized being worshipped by her partner and another man. One man can penetrate her while the other receives a blowjob from her.

A great way to make this fantasy a reality is to join a local swinger club. Couples are encouraged to live out their fantasies there!

Exhibitionism:

Some sort of public sex-whether it be filming a porno between you and your partner-or fucking in a public place are fantasies all men and women are likely to have at some point in their lives.

Filming a porno is not recommended for obvious reasons. While it is legal it can have serious professional consequences if your friends/families/coworkers find out! Having sex in a public area is a much more commonly fulfilled fantasy. However-use with caution and make sure you don't get caught, as this can have serious legal consequences! Read on in chapter 5 for some awesome places to have sex.

Strap on sex:

This is a fantasy held by women where they play the "man" for the night and wear a "strap-on" penis. Both the woman and even the man have fun with this-as the woman will enjoy being the aggressor for the night and penetrating the man. Having her man vulnerable to this kind of sex is an incredible turn-on for women. You can purchase a strap-on penis at a local adult store.

Rough sex:

Rough sex is awesome. Rough sex is tolerable pain added to sex to increase pleasure and turn-ons.

Here are a few tips on how you can "rough-it-up" in the bedroom:

1. Scream and yell

2. Nibble and bite (gently). This is great for erogenous zones such as the vagina, balls, penis, breasts, perineum (the area between the butthole and the balls or vagina), the neck, belly, and inner thighs.

3. Claw your lover (again, gently).

4. Aggressive movements. Pounding and fucking each other aggressively like there's no tomorrow will turn you two on like nothing else.

5. Pulling each other's hair.

6. Slapping each other. A light slap across the face or your partner's butt is great for this.

7. Abusive dirty talk. Read my books on talking dirty for more about this! But saying to each other "fuck me like you hate me" or "call me a bitch!" are huge turn-ons.

8. Forcing your partner to perform sexual acts. For example, shoving your cock down your woman's throat is great for this.

9. Spanking.

10. Dominance and submission.

11. Sex toys and gags.

Cumming all over your woman's face and squirting all over your man's body:

Both sexes fantasize about their partner releasing all their juices all over their faces/bodies.

Sitting on your partner's face:

For women: your man has fantasized about you sitting on his face so he can eat your pussy out. They also fantasize about getting a face rub from your pussy as you sit on their face, rotate your hips around so your pussy and butthole gets rubbed all over his face and mouth.

For men: your woman has fantasized about a similar face rub from you. Sitting on your woman's face and rubbing your penis, balls, and butthole against her mouth and face is a huge turn on.

These are all just fantasies....but all are very doable and will make your sex life adventurous. Talk to your partner and give some of them a try!

Chapter 4 – Sex Bucket list ideas

It's normal and understandable for things to get "stale" in a long-term couple's relationship regarding sex. A great way to avoid that is to come up with a "sex bucket list" of some naughty and kinky ideas for sex.

Here are some great sex bucket list items to add to your list:

<u>**Your Sex Bucket List:**</u>

Have "Everything but" Sex:

When you first began your long term relationship with your partner, you sometimes had make-out sessions that lasted for several hours-but did not go any further. Those sessions often die down after a relationship has lasted several years-where the intense kissing and touching goes away. Try "Everything but" sex where you focus just on all the kissing, touching, and groping that comes beforehand!

Have "Sense-sational" sex:

This type of sex involved removing one of the five senses. For example, wear a blindfold during your sex session and let your partner have his/her way with you-or wear earplugs and have "silent sex". What this does is it cancels out one or two senses but causes your other senses (i.e. touch) and arousals/feelings to amplify-creating an amazing moment between you two.

Have "just because" Sex:

Unplanned sex for no reason other than for the sake of having sex "just because". For no reason at all remove your clothes and your partner will likely do the same. Do it then and there.

Shower Sex:

Fucking your partner against a wall in a shower can be dangerous if your floor is too slippery-therefore be careful. However-if done right this can be fun! Having sex with warm water pouring over you feels great.

Tie your partner up or be tied up:

For more information about this-you should check out my upcoming book on BDSM practices and moves. But to summarize, men and women both fantasize about being the dominant and the dominated during sex. There is something inherently sexy about being tied up and submitting control to your partner and letting him/her have their way with you however they please! Try this out!

Sex in a car:

A parked car-of course! And make sure it's your car and not someone else's!

Food Sex:

Why eat your dinner off of platters and silverware when you can eat off of each other's naked bodies? Give this a try every now and then. Good foods to incorporate with sex are: chocolate, strawberries, bananas, whipped cream, cherries, melons, ice cream, bacon, and champagne.

"We Might Just Get Caught" Sex:

We talk more about some awesome locations to have sex next chapter-but both men and women fantasize about having sex in an area where they "might just get caught". The thrill adds to the arousal and makes it so much more fun!

Video Tape yourselves having sex:

This is always a fun way for you and your partner to watch each other fuck each other in your own homemade porno for you and your partner's eyes only. However-be careful where you store this! Make sure no one else will see it, and definitely don't let it end up on the Internet!

Multiple Orgasms Sex:

Have sex for several hours with the ultimate goal as to make your woman orgasm and your man cum at least 3-5 times.

24 hour sex marathon:

Pick a day where both you and your partner have a 100% clear schedule. Be naked with each other all day and fuck each other's brains out all day. You can have normal sex all day, but you can also try many of the bucket list items in this book at multiple locations during that day. This just may be the ultimate sex bucket list item.

Weekend long sex marathon:

This is basically the same as the previous one-except for an entire weekend! Pick a weekend where from Friday evening until Sunday night you and your partner have an empty schedule and implement a no-clothes rule for the entire weekend. Other than sleeping for eight hours on Friday night and Saturday night-nonstop sex is a must for the rest of the weekend!

Tantric Sex:

Check out my book on Tantra Sex for more information about this!

Sensual Massage:

Give your partner a sensual massage while he or she is naked. There is nothing more relaxing than having your partner gently and sensually rubbing oil all around your naked body and genitals.

Other Tips to Consider:

Start using Sex toys:

Sex toys are a great way to make your sex life more kinky. Women love vibrators. Don't be embarrassed to go into an adult store to purchase sex toys. The clerks have seen it all!

Read Erotica Novels and Watch Porn with your partner:

Every since 50 Shades of Grey became popular-many short erotica novels have hit bestseller status on amazon. Reading these along with your partner (and even reenacting scenes) is a great way to keep you and your partner horny for each other and constantly come up with new ideas.

Porn is a great way to come up with new ideas too. Most porn sites (as you probably know) are free and don't require a membership.

Talk Dirty to Each other:

Check out my two books one Dirty Talk about this. But summary-you want to explore dirty talk-as it is hot and builds up anticipation for sex.

Watch movies with steamy sex scenes:

This reiterates the previous idea-but it is important that you two are always on the lookout for new ideas!

For women-wear slutty lingerie more often:

This is great for foreplay. If you beat your partner home from work-surprise him at the door with a slutty outfit that reveals!

Don't just do it in the bedroom:

You have an entire house or apartment. Use every inch of it!

Sext each other more often:

I have an upcoming book on Sexting. This is a great way to get each other aroused and in anticipation for sex.

<u>Final Bucket List items:</u>

1	Pitch black sex
3	Have anal
4	Have a threesome
5	Have group sex at a swingers club
6	Voyeurism (watching others have sex!)
7	Completely silent sex
8	Teasing your partner to the point of orgasm!
9	Sex in a tent
10	Sexual role play
11	For women: double penetration with a dildo and your man at the same time

12   Have sex with your partner while someone else is watching

13   Very loud sex

14   Masturbate together

15   Making out with no sex long after you're no longer a virgin

16   A quickie in a skirt in a public area

17   Sex on the floor

18   Sex with no break in eye contact

19   Sending naked photos to each another

20   Broad daylight sex

21   Play strip chess

Chapter 5 – Awesome places to have sex

Think about all the wildest and craziest places that you fantasized about having sex. Make it a reality! Relationship expert Emily Morse, Ph. D., says that expanding your sexual experiences outside of the bedroom leads to more spontaneity and more closeness with your partner. Great sex experiences are great for conversation with your partner and are great for making good memories with your partner.

Getting it on in different places is more about the new and exciting experiences you will have with your partner and not just about orgasm or ejaculation. By having new sex experiences in different places-you will learn more about yourself and what turns you and your partner on.

Many of the below locations are public-so use with caution!

Awesome place to have sex with your partner:

Your backyard: having sex in the backyard is a great place to get it on when you don't want to have to worry about getting caught but still want to do it outside.

The couch: fucking your woman on the couch with multiple pillows under your woman's back can increase the likelihood of orgasm.

Hotel Sex: A hotel has all the benefits of sex with none of the normal responsibilities of being an adult. You don't have to worry about making the bed or clean up-as housekeeping takes care of that. Plus-if you ever want to have crazy loud sex so that your kids won't hear-a hotel is a great place to go for an offsite fuckfest!

A public event: Weddings, sports events, parties, etc. This adds to the thrill of "we just might get caught." Definitely do this one when you want that excitement to be really high. Find a bathroom or a closet farthest away from the crowd.

If you only have a few minutes, this is a great opportunities to give her a quickie through her skirt-as this is easy to cover up if someone is coming!

Mirror Sex: Sex in front of the mirror is a huge turn on for women because she can see how she looks while jumping your bones.

On the Beach: This inherently is one of the most romantic places to have sex. However, make sure to do it on a towel-as you don't want sand getting in your vagina or butthole.

An Empty College Classroom or Library: This is a naughty one. Check the class or library hours to make sure you won't get interrupted. It is recommended that she wears a skirt or dress with no panties just to make the "in and out" easier.

A Park: Look for a beautiful park to do this on. Bring a tent or blanket with you!

An elevator: This one is naughty too and the risk of getting caught is high. However, its extremely hot. I would recommend saving this one for buildings or locations that aren't that busy. Make sure there isn't a security camera in the elevator!

A closet: Whether it be a party, event, or even at a friends house-fucking in a closet is hot.

A Jacuzzi: Book a room with a Jacuzzi if you don't own one. This too is one of the more romantic locations to get it on.

A limousine: This is great if you are having a limousine transport you somewhere and you can't keep your hands off each other during the ride. Make sure that the privacy window is down though.... Don't distract the driver!

A waterbed: This is a step up from regular sex in the bed. The slip and slide makes things rougher and more fun.

Private office party: If you have keys to a private office-show your partner how hard you work on that desk (in a different way).

A boat: Getting it on with waves in the background is awesome.

On a roof: This is still outside yet still gives you some privacy. However-don't be too loud!

The woods: It is beautiful to have sex where there is nothing but nature all around you. However, this is exciting and thrilling-because you never know if someone will walk by!

Tantra Sex:

The Beginner's Guide to 25 Tantra Techniques

information is without contract or any type of guarantee assurance.

The trademarks that are used are without any consent, and the publication of the trademark is without permission or backing by the trademark owner. All trademarks and brands within this book are for clarifying purposes only and are the owned by the owners themselves, not affiliated with this document.

Introduction

I want to thank you and congratulate you for downloading the book, *"Tantra Sex: The Beginner's Guide to 25 Tantra Techniques (tantra, sex positions, sex guide, bedroom, sex life, orgasm, sex in marriage, erotic, kinky)"*.

This book contains proven steps and strategies on how to practice tantric sex and enjoy all its benefits. If you want to have a deeper connection with your partner and make your sex life more intense and exciting, this is definitely the right book to read.

Here's a quick overview of what this book offers:

-Understand tantric sex and its powerful benefits

-Learn how it can help your relationship

-Find out the best techniques to spice things up in the bedroom

-Explore new ways to please your lover

-Discover how you can have a lasting and unforgettable experience in different positions

-Find out how you can last longer in bed

-Learn how to have a full body orgasm

If you are ready to create waves in your sex life, read on!

Thanks again for downloading this book, I hope you enjoy it!

Chapter 1 – Tantric Sex and Its Intense Benefits

What's all the fuss about tantric sex anyway? What makes so many couples crazy over Tantra? Is it that good? If you're wondering and asking these questions, it is due time to satisfy your curiosity and have an experience like no other.

So What Is Tantra?

An ancient practice from the Hindi, tantric sex is translated as "the weaving and expansion of energy." And this is exactly how you will feel during a session. Unlike regular sex or what most people are used to engaging in, Tantra encourages a slow rhythm. Because we do things in a rush including the sexual act, we forget to appreciate the most important things in our lives like intimacy. Tantric sex aims to bring romance and intimacy back. This is why many couples including Sting and his wife Trudy practice Tantra.

Tantric sex can help enhance intimacy between two people. In Tantra, the sexual act is not just the connection of bodies, it is also about the connection of minds. With tantric sex, you are promised of enhanced intimacy and stronger connection. With this increased romance between the couple, a powerful orgasm can be experienced.

You can think of it this way. A quick sex is a fast food meal that you eat on the sidewalk. It may taste good and it will fill you up. You may not mind having it on the sidewalk because you were able to satisfy your hunger. Now think of tantric sex as gourmet meal prepared by a top chef. You can enjoy the delicious smelling, mouth-watering dish in a cozy restaurant with soothing music, relaxed and sophisticated vibe. Each bite colors your palette. It is an explosion of wonderful flavors that sends fireworks in your mind. It is more than satisfying. It is an unforgettable experience! That's tantric sex.

Tantric sex engages all your senses. It involves every inch of your body. Tantra makes the most use of the power of touch and the intensity of eye contact, the union of breathing and the slow thrusting to bring you a full body orgasm.

The Intense Benefits of Tantric Sex

Tantric sex has all the physical benefits of regular sex. It is good for the immune system and it also helps in calorie burning. It can aid in relieving pain and it can help you age more gracefully. The calming effect of orgasm can also reduce your risk to depression. The difference is in tantric sex, the release of 'happy' chemicals responsible for all these health benefits is much greater. It is prolonged and intensified.

Also, you will greatly benefit from practicing tantric sex if you want to rekindle romance in your love life. Tantric sex can bring back the spark between couples who have been together for a long time. That's because it can bring you two together in unison. It can enhance your intimacy. It helps you reconnect with each other not only physically but also mentally and emotionally.

With Tantra, the focus is not the end goal. Rather, more emphasis is given on the journey. It commits you to the present to make you feel every bit of sensation, savor every moment and allow the pleasure to tingle every part of your body.

Are you ready to have a different kind of experience, one that brings you to pure ecstasy? If you are then you better read on!

Chapter 2 – 25 Powerful Tantric Sex Techniques

Sex is a powerful and satisfying experience. If you want to take it to the next level though and create a sensation so intense it creates ripples throughout your bodies and at the same time rekindle romance between you and your beloved, you can try the following techniques.

1. Create an intimacy space.

The bedroom should only serve two purposes: for sleeping and lovemaking. With this said, you need to get rid of the clutter. Take advantage of the opportunity to turn your room into something with a relaxing environment and playful vibe.

Lighting is important. Make sure it is romantic. Dim the lights or use candles. Use cozy fabrics and soft sheets for your bed. Everything should be clean. The environment should put you both at ease.

2. Tease the senses with sensual scents.

Did you know that there are specific smells that can trigger sensual responses in both men and women? These scents can both have a relaxing and aphrodisiac effect. So what are these romantic scents?

Vanilla -Men and women have relied on this scent for centuries to spice things up in the bedroom. In fact, there is reason to believe that even Thomas Jefferson himself, who was responsible for bringing vanilla to the United States, used the spice to help with his love life.

Jasmine -The sweet and soothing scent of jasmine is charming. It is believed to help in relieving tension and preparing lovers for romance.

Licorice and Cucumber —Now licorice and cucumber seem like an unusual combination. Although they don't sound sexy, they are scientifically proven to stir sexual arousal in both sexes.

Banana Nut Bread -This smell proves to be just as effective as licorice and cucumber in stirring a sensual response. If you're wondering how to make this smell, why not bake some so you have a delicious dessert and an enticing aroma to get you and your lover in the mood for love.

Peppermint -Used in the right quantity, peppermint can help with your sex life. If your breath smells fresh, your partner will be more enticed to kiss you.

Other scents worthy of mention are ylang ylang, rose, sandalwood, patchouli, neroli, vetiver, and clary sage, among others. You can get these scents in aromatherapy shops in the form of soaps, candles, air fresheners, etc.

3. Take a relaxing bath.

Prepare a bubble bath for you and your lover. Use scented soaps. Adorn the bathroom with candles. Spread rose petals over the bath and on the floor. You don't have to use a scrub. You can use your hands to gently run the soap or soapy water all over each other's body. No kissing yet. Focus on touching each other's body gently.

You can also prepare a glass of wine or a cup of tea. This will help further in easing tension in your bodies and relaxing your senses.

4. Play your song/s.

Create a romantic soundtrack. Choose songs that you both like and mean something in your relationship. Play it softly in the background. Remember, these songs should help you connect with each other. They should not, in any way, disrupt the mood. Make sure the music plays continuously at least for 2 to 3 hours so your session won't be interrupted with the need to replay the tunes.

5. Use a blindfold.

After the soothing bath, pat your bodies dry and put on a comfortable robe. Lead your partner into the bedroom. Tie a silk scarf to use as blindfold. Slowly guide him/ her into your temple of love.

Why is this important? This is part of the foreplay. You are teasing your lover's senses. This is the time to focus on other senses other than sight. It can make his other senses more sensitive like his sense of touch and smell.

6. Make your lover smell romance.

Guide your partner into the bed and sit him/ her comfortably on the bed. With the blindfold still on, hold a scented item under your lover's nose. We've talked about sensual scents earlier. Use the scents you prepared.

Hold the item under your partner's nose for 10 to 15 seconds. Prepare 5 to 6 different scents. Focus on light, romantic scents and steer clear of those that may irritate rather than relax your lover.

7. Tease him/ her with textures.

Lay him down on his stomach. At this point, you can remove the blindfold and your robes. As your lover relaxes into position, put your hand on his back. With your other hand, hold a firm textured item and run it gently through his body. Start from your lover's left shoulder down to his back to his leg to the left foot. Do it slowly and gently. Then, run the firm textured item again from his right shoulder all the way down to his right foot.

It is important that you take your time so your lover can enjoy the sensation. It is also important that you pay particular attention to his responses. This is for you to know what feels comfortable or what he seems to enjoy the most. Respond to his bodily cues. Stay longer to areas that make your lover feel more relaxed and those he feels more pleasure at. Run the firm textured item to both sides of your lover's body several times, at least three but not more than six times.

With one hand still on your lover's back, take a soft-textured item on the other hand to run through his body. Stroke your lover gently with this soft textured item from the shoulders to the feet. Do it slowly and gently. Repeat the gentle stroking several times before switching back to a firm or rough textured item.

For the rough or firm textured item, you can use a warm stone, a stick or a spiked massager. You can even use your nails. For the soft-textured item, you can prepare a feather or the silk scarf you used as blindfold. Women can even use their hair. Prepare at least two different rough and soft textured items. Alternately stroke your lover's body with these items for 15 to 20 minutes.

8. Give your lover a full body tantric massage.

You don't have to be a professional masseuse to do this. Work on your lover's body by instinct. Consider his responses and adjust your strokes accordingly. Apply more or less pressure as needed. Focus on what seems to make him feel good. Do not engage the spine. It is best to start by applying light strokes then you can increase the pressure depending in his response.

Use your palms for gentle strokes and switch to the heels of your hands to increase the pressure. Broad strokes are ideal in some areas while circular motions are best for others.

Pour a generous amount of oil on your hands first. Make sure they are warm before you touch your lover's body. You can also pour oil over the body part you are about to massage. The pouring of oil on his back for instance, can give your partner a sensual sensation.

Give your lover a full body massage focusing on one area at a time. You can give the massage using the following order.

Neck and shoulders -Start from the center of the neck to the shoulders down to the arms.

Side of spine -Again, you should avoid applying direct pressure to the spine. Rather, you should focus on the side, left and right. Apply continuous movement from below the shoulders to the hips. Work on this area for at least ten minutes.

Back of the legs -No kneading in this area please, it's a big yes however, to firm and slow strokes.

Gently place your left hand over your partner's tailbone and your right hand on the back of his head. Take deep and long breathes together before you ask him to turn over.

Feet -Touching the feet creates an unbelievable sensation because this area is filled with nerve endings. You can use your thumbs to stroke your partner's feet but if he is ticklish, you can also use your palms. Start with the back of his toes then at the back of the foot. Be careful not to press too hard on the arch of the feet. Work your way from his toes to the heel. Take your time to allow your lover to enjoy the sensation.

Front of the Legs -Front the foot, slide your hands over to his ankles and thighs.

Belly -Keep your hands flat while you apply a clockwise circular motion. Focus on giving your partner comforting, gentle and slow strokes. Allot at least 3 minutes to this area.

Chest -Apply tender pressure in this area. Experiment with different strokes. Work on the lymph nodes and the nipples gently.

Head and shoulders -From the chest, move your hands to the head. Gently massage the scalp then move on to his forehead and brow area.

Arms -Apply firm and long strokes from your lover's shoulders to his wrist. A little kneading technique is allowed in this area.

9. **Make eye contact.**

As you are touching and stroking your partner, maintain eye contact. Look into his eyes as you lovingly caress his body. Remember that Tantra is all about creating intimacy. It is about union. Nothing is more intimate than gazing into each other's eyes as you make each other feel different kinds of sensations. It keeps you connected and engaged with one another throughout the entire process. This is one of the things that make tantric massage more intimate, pleasurable and satisfying more than others.

10.   Do the hand-slide.

There are different kinds of strokes you can try as you caress your lover's body. One of which is the hand slide technique. All you need to do is slide your hands up and down his/ her body parallel to each other. You can apply this technique as you massage your beloved's sides, lower back and buttocks. As you move your hands together back to his shoulders, continue the sliding motion to his neck, arms and fingertips. From the fingertips, arms, neck and shoulders, slide down to his back, sides, hip and buttocks again. Repeat the movement at least six times.

11. Try the pull-ups for variation.

The massage should be about giving pleasure and so it is essential that you experiment with different kinds of techniques. And this is another variation you can try.

You can begin by moving the palms of your hands together stroking his sides. Then you can gently pull up the flesh on his sides to the waist and hips. When your over turns over, gently pull up the sides of his chest towards his spine. Slowly slide your hands to the arms and pull them up towards the spine.

Do it gently. Alternate the sliding stroke with the pull ups. This technique can create intensity and a more pleasurable sensation for your partner.

12.　　Knead your lover's fleshy parts.

Some body parts are better treated with broad, long strokes. Others however, can take more pressure through kneading like the buttocks. Squeeze into your lover's buttocks using your thumbs and fingers. Use a flowing motion.

Do it alternately with your hands. Then, to mix it up you can slide your hands up to the side of the spine to shoulders and back down, knead again, slide down the hips, thighs and legs, back up and knead again. You may also spread the cheeks gently as you apply a kneading motion. The changes in pressure and stroke can create an exciting sensation for your partner.

13.　　Use a feather stroke.

You can also caress your beloved's skin with your fingertips. Create a light feather stroke as you touch his neck, shoulders, arms, back, buttocks, thighs and legs. Use either a circular motion or long fluid ones.

Work on his body from side to side, up and down. Start with light strokes. Apply more pressure like a gentle scratch gradually. Make sure you have enough oil on your hands and on his body so the scratch won't bruise his skin.

14.   Give your man a lingam massage.

Start by pouring oil on his shaft and testicles. Stroke them gently. Smoothly slide your hands to his scrotum. Apply slow but firm strokes. Then, massage the area between his testicles and anus. Gently push the area. Take your time in these areas before you start stroking his shaft.

Gently squeeze the base of the lingam and slowly pull up along the shaft. Let your hands slide down smoothly. Switch hands each time. Do not rush the process. You can then work on the head of the lingam. Squeeze on it and slide down like squeezing juice out of an orange in a manual juicer. Try applying circular strokes too from the head to shaft.

Don't use a timer for this process. Instead, take cues from him. You will know when to stop as his body will tell you. Let him rest for a little while before you proceed again.

15.Give your woman a yoni massage.

Pour a generous amount of oil on the yoni. Let it drop from the mound to the outer lips. Put one hand on the outer area of the yoni and use the dominant hand to stroke the mound and the outer lips. Slide up and down with your thumb and index finger slowly entering the inner lips. Use varying amounts of pressure and speed.

Stroke the clitoris gently in a clockwise and counter-clockwise motion. Squeeze on it lightly. As you are working on caressing the clitoris, enter the yoni and explore it with your finger. Move your finger gently up and down, sideways and in circles. Tease her inside by motioning 'come here' with your middle finger. It will tickle her G-spot and give her a powerful experience. Continue experimenting with various strokes, speed and pressure. When she is peaking, slow down and let the energy subside before you create another wave of sensation massaging the yoni.

16.   Meditate together.

After the massage, take your time to connect with each other and be as one. Take a seating position with your legs crossed, facing each other. Hold each other's hand and close your eyes.

17. Sit in silence and start breathing deeply.

Breathe in deeply through the mouth and breathe out slowly through the nose. Adjust to each other's phase until you create a rhythm. Breathe together in silence and be aware of nothing else but the touch of each other's hands, your presence and the rhythm of your breathing.

This exercise helps you both get rid of your worries and bring each other to the present. When you are both fully present, you are more capable of focusing on each other.

18.   Awaken each other's nerve endings.

Maintain eye contact and your seating position, cross legged and facing each other. Move your palm or fingertips all over his body, just above the surface. Don't touch him yet. The purpose of this exercise is to awaken the nerves through a tingling sensation as you feel each other's hand over your skin but not really touching.

Tease your lover with long strokes moving throughout his body. Crush as close as you can to the breast and privates, taking great care not to touch his skin. When you're done, ask your lover to do the same to you.

19.   Massage yourselves.

You can do this part together. Instead of massaging each other, massage your own bodies. This is done in preparation for tantric sex. It involves awakening the nine chakras. Ask your partner to follow your lead. Massage each part of the body in multiples of nine breaths.

Begin by gently massaging your breasts in a circular motion then slowly move your fingers to caress your nipples. Do this for nine breaths. From the breast, move your fingers to the rib section. Again, use a spiraling motion to massage the area. This time, do it for 18 breaths. Continue the same massaging motion with the rest of the areas, increasing breaths by 9 each time you go further down. Here's the sequence.

-Breast and nipples for 9 breaths

-Ribs for 18 breaths

-End of the ribs for 27 breaths

-Between ribs and navel for 36 breaths

-With both hands, below the navel for 45 breaths

-Between your navel and pubic bone for 54 breaths

-Pubic bone for 63 breaths

-Privates for 72 breaths

-Behind your genitals for 81 breaths

Take slow deep breaths. It's not a race. Finish together.

20.   Awaken each other's kundalini.

Sexual energy rests within us. Through massage and focusing on desires, this intense sexual energy will be awakened. It will grow as your desires intensify.

To begin, the female partner should position herself behind her man. Sit close enough so that the breasts touch the back of the man. Remember the nine areas massaged in multiples of nine in the previous technique. You are now about to do the massage for each other.

Follow the same sequence, the same spiraling movement and the same count as you move from the breast and nipples down. After the massage is completed, take turns. The male partner should now sit behind his woman.

21.   Increase the arousal.

Sit with you and your lover's back touching. Sit closely to make your buttocks touch as well. Place one hand on your own heart. Use the other to touch your own privates. Sway gently in unison. Move back and forth and take deep breaths. Close your eyes. Free your mind of any thoughts. Focus on your sexual desires. Feel the sensation of the slow rocking. Feel the rhythm you are creating together. Maintain the slow and steady pace.

Next, rotate your waists together with your hands still in place. Do this slowly as you feel the sexual energy filling you up. It will make you feel a force so intense. Do not stop. Build up the pace and slow down again. After this, you can lie down together to rest and let the sexual energy fade a little.

22.   Unite your sexual energies.

When you're ready, sit facing each other. Allow your knees to touch. Place one hand on your own heart. Gently caress your privates using the other hand. Do the same motion, back and forth then a circular motion. Sway together and maintain eye contact. Breathe deeply as your sexual energies unite and travel in waves throughout your bodies.

23.   Sit in a yab yum pose.

It is one of the traditional tantric poses which promote intimacy and intense connection between couples. The man should be seating down with his legs crossed. The woman will then sit on top of her beloved's legs. Facing and embracing each other, breathe in and out fully, always together. Take your time to let your bodies tune in to this loving embrace. Look into each other's eyes.

Sit still and feel the warmth of each other's body. Look at each other feel the love and affection between you. Appreciate the moment you are sharing. Realize how special it is. Allow yourselves to be filled up with joy as you celebrate your togetherness.

24.   Say what you love about each other.

Still in a yab yum pose and maintaining eye contact, start saying what you love and appreciate about each other. Use a loving and gentle tone. Pronounce each word. Take each other's words in. Be honest and authentic as much as you can. This should be more about sharing, receiving and giving. Express yourself. Reach deep into each other's hearts. Take turns in speaking.

Don't rush. Always speak from the heart. You can start your sentences with the following phrases.

"I really appreciate..."

"I truly love..."

"My heart deeply desires..."

"It brings me joy when you..."

"You make me feel pleasure when you..."

After the moment of sharing, thank each other.

25.   Share a slow and sensual kiss.

Maintaining the yab yum pose, breathe together in harmony. Breathe each other's breath while looking at each other in the eyes lovingly. Softly and gently join your lips.

Resist the temptation to be aggressive. Simply enjoy the sensation as you caress your lover's lips with your own and his/ her on yours. Relax and savor the moment. Enjoy the closeness of your bodies. Be completely in the present.

Chapter 3 – Ultimate Tantric Sex Positions

Neither you nor your partner has to be an extortionist to have a taste of tantric sex. Tantric sex after all, is not about getting on complex, uncomfortable positions. Rather, it is all about enjoying togetherness and enhancing intimacy. This way, you and your lover can experience a much higher level of satisfaction.

Awaken the intense energy within you and connect with your partner deeply with tantric positions. You can start with the yab yum position described in the previous chapter and proceed with any of the following.

The Missionary

A classic, this is probably one of the most intimate sex positions. The man is in full control. It is great for tantric sex because it allows the couple to look into each other's eyes and sensually kiss. While the man sets the pace, the woman can put her hands on her partner's hips to guide him to go deeper or slower. The woman can also move her hips as her lover moves   with   her.

Valedictorian

A variation of the missionary position, the valedictorian also encourages eye contact. The advantage is that the woman's ankles rest on the man's shoulders so her legs make a "V." This position allows deeper penetration.

The Hot Seat

The man kneels behind the woman. The woman kneels in front of the man, placing her legs between his. Both bodies are tightly squeezed together. The man puts his hands on the waist, hips or forearms. The woman holds on to the man's hips. They move up and down in unison or move their hips in circular motion. For better access to the woman's G-spot, the man should lean slightly backwards.

Sexy Back

The man kneels and sits on his heels. The woman lowers her body in a squat putting her legs on the side of his. The woman rests her hands on her thighs for support. The man can also place his hands on the woman's rear to provide her support.

In this position, the woman is completely in charge. While the full rear view of the woman is satisfying in itself, it can be sexier for both when it is done in front of a mirror.

Spooning

Just as if not more intimate than the missionary, spooning provides couples a chance to be more affectionate with each other. It gives the man complete access to the woman's body. The woman can also twist her head and body slightly toward the man so they can share a sensual kiss during the act. It also makes a perfect position for snuggling after both reach the climax.

The Sidewinder

The woman is on her side with one of her legs resting on the man's shoulder. The man hugs his woman's legs and straddles her bottom thigh. This L-shape position creates a powerful stimulation. Because the pelvises are close together, the man has an opportunity to enter the woman at various angles.

Rocking Chair

While the man lies on his back, the woman straddles him slowly. After entering the woman, the man raises his torso. He wraps his legs tightly around the woman's buttocks and the woman does the same. Their elbows are placed under each other's knees and raise them to chest level. They cradle each other back and forth.

To make up for the difficulty of this position, the couple can take turns kissing each other's neck or playing on the other's earlobes. A tip for women, tighten your PC muscles. This will increase blood flow which leads to more pleasure for you both.

The Lap Dance

The man sits on a tall-backed chair, padded with pillows while the woman moves in position to straddle him. She slightly leans back holding on his knees for support. Her legs are extended so her ankles can rest on the man's shoulders. For this to work, the woman must find a way to balance her weight between her hands and ankles.

Because the woman does most of the pumping, she can speed it up and slow her pace when her man is close to climax. This way, she can make him last longer so they can share more intimate moments together.

The Mermaid

The woman lies on her back at the edge of the bed or desk. Her buttocks are slightly elevated by a pillow. With her legs straight up, the man moves in and enters her standing up.

Because the woman's legs are together, it makes her man feel more friction. She can also separate her legs and keep them together again so her man can feel the tightness sending him into a pleasurable rush.

The Butterfly

As the woman lies on the edge of the bed or desk, her man takes her by the hips to penetrate her. She then rests her legs on his shoulders so he can thrust into her more deeply and vigorously. She can hold at the edge of the desk or free a hand so she can stimulate her clitoris. Watching her do this, her man can get even more excited.

Row the Boat

It's no secret. Men like women on top. Row the Boat is a variation of the woman on top but with an exciting twist. While the man relaxes on a reclining chair, she straddles his lap. With her knees bent and her man's tight grip on her buttocks, she moves up and down.

The up and down motion along a man's shaft creates excitement but she can turn things up even more by making circular motions with her hips. Because this position allows the couple to look at each other, it creates an intimate moment but engages their primal desires at the same time.

G Force

The woman lies on her back with her knees close to her chest. The man moves in kneeling and grabbing her feet. She thrusts her hips forward to allow him to enter. She rests her feet on his chest and he holds on to her hips.

This position allows the man to plunge into her deeper and farther. To make it more pleasurable for his woman, he can stimulate her clitoris and send her to pure bliss.

The Pretzel

Kneeling face to face, the couple are joined together equally putting in the effort to create a back and forth rhythm. Although the position doesn't give much room for deep penetration, it does give the couples a chance to pay attention to other body parts. With their hands available, they can feel free to explore each other's bodies.

Chapter 4 - Additional Tips for Intensifying Sex Life

If you want to make the most of your time together and make it more special, you can follow these additional tips for a more blissful experience.

Allow each other to enjoy every moment.

Pay attention on how the sensation makes you feel, the tingling not only in the area that connects you to your partner but also everywhere else. Give as much as you receive. Make the effort to please your partner and trust that he/ she will do the same.

Do it slowly.

Just because foreplay is over does not mean you should cross the finish line in a hurry. Remember, it is not a race. The journey is much more important than the destination.

Build it up slowly.

Allow the penetration to happen smoothly and effortlessly. Begin with slow and shallow thrusts. Do not just focus on the genitals. Whenever your hands are free to roam, explore your partner's body. Caress his back. Look into each other's eyes. Feel the vibration each thrust creates. Notice the sensation it sends throughout your body.

Steady your breathing.

Breathing slowly and steadily can help you and your partner last longer. What usually happens is, people tense up and breathe faster when they are peaking. While this can lead to orgasm, it can also rob you of the opportunity to experience a much more intense 'O.' So relax and take slow deep breaths together as you build up to a mind blowing orgasm.

Build up and back down.

Want to know how to have a full body orgasm? Aside from breathing slowly and steadily, you can also intensify the orgasm for you and your lover by slowly building up the excitement and allowing it to fade a little when you feel each other's erotic energy reach a peaking point.

When the excitement subsides, start slowly again. Do not allow each other to completely go over the edge until both of you are ready to let go of the moment you are sharing. You can play on this build up and slowing down for as long as you like. When you are ready, you can have a final orgasm that creates ripple throughout your bodies.

Finally, you should always end with a gentle kiss and a warm embrace.

Talking Dirty for Men:
How to Get Your Girl Aroused and in the Mood for Sex!

Introduction

There are plenty of reasons why couples need to talk dirty to each other. But the top one would be because the both of you need to know what the other person is comfortable doing. Let's say that there is a sex position that one person wants that they have never tried before. If they are to ever get their partner in the mood to give it a shot, they are going to have to be open and honest about their desires, and not be afraid if their partner is hesitant. But there is no way to know how comfortable they are or will be unless you voice it.

It's always going to be to your benefit to keep your partner aware of what is going on. Surprises are good, but not always. You don't want to sneak something in on them that they are not ready for just because you think it is sexy, and that goes for women as well as men. But this book is for the fellas, so it's important to know guys that one bad decision could mean the difference between a night of passion and you ruining the mood. Keeping your lover in the loop with great dirty talk is what the following chapters are all about. There will be 200 examples of dirty talk numbered throughout the book, so watch as the number increases. Enjoy!

Chapter 1: Why Couples Need Dirty Talk

When you talk dirty in bed, it brings about spontaneous ideas that you never thought were there. Simply living in the moment can spark up something new and fresh that you didn't even think was available. The moment the sensual words leave your lips the chances of your creative juices starting to flow increases greatly. But believe me, if the moment is hot enough, those are not the only juices that will begin to flow, and as you and your partner begin to trade off ideas you'll realize that you really aren't planning anything at all...it'll feel natural to talk dirty.

Probably one of the best reasons to talk dirty in bed is because it is wonderful for foreplay. Sure, there may be other ways that you do it for your partner, especially if you know them and have been together for a long time. You know where to touch them to make them hot, but if you choose the right words at the right time there will be an increased intenseness that you weren't aware of before. Choosing the right words can make an already hot foreplay routine ten times better.

When you aren't afraid to talk dirty to your partner, and really open up, you'll see a side of you that you didn't before. Your words will be coming from a place that is not planned or proper or grammatically correct, or anything near what you can say in public. You will be saying exactly what you are doing or want to do right in the moment, and you will undoubtedly at some moments surprise yourself. This is especially true if you have just started to experiment with talking dirty. You may end up going into a direction that you never imagined with your partner.

The key to talking dirty is to give it an element of surprise. Although you should not surprise your partner with an actual act without explaining first, you can always safely surprise them with your words. The key is to not overdo it when you are not in bed, because it could take away from the intimate moments between the sheets. Don't bed-talk in the car, in the kitchen, or anywhere else public, unless of course you and your partner are adventurous and are purposefully trying to arouse yourselves in these places. I'm not telling you to have sex in public, although some do find it quite erotic!

Talking dirty in bed will always lead up to better sex. What's the best part about it is you do not have to master it to make it work for you. In fact, when you say exactly what's on your mind, some of the funniest things will come out of your mouths, and you'll sometimes find yourselves laughing out loud as you challenge each other to go back and forth saying the dirtiest lines the both of you can think of. Sex is supposed to be happy, and you'll see just what I mean when you find that talking dirty is a much needed thing.

Chapter 2: Talking Dirty Without Feeling Awkward

Sometimes the reason some people don't talk dirty is because they just feel really weird doing it. They aren't used to actually saying what they want although there is no doubt in their mind that they want it. There are a few ways that you can get better at it if you feel that you could use some guidance. But you will soon find as you read on that there is no really perfect way to talk dirty. The biggest steps are figuring out when to do it and what you find are the biggest turn-ons for your partner.

One thing you should never do is try to be something or someone that you are not when talking dirty. I want to be clear on this point, though, because there are those couples out there who roleplay. If you are in character, then yes, go ahead and play your role and be someone that you are not! But if you are not actually acting out a character and being extra kinky that day, then it is always best to not come across as fake. Be yourself, and talk to them when you say dirty things that reflects your natural tone of voice, especially if you are whispering it in their ears.

When you remain honest, the natural way you feel will come out and your partner will feel that you are being genuine and real when you say the things that you do. It is not good if your words come across as forced – it will make it look like you are *trying* to talk dirty instead of simply talking dirty. For example, you could repeat a scene from the night before sometime when she won't expect it the following day. When you feel she is not thinking about it, walk over to her and whisper how you loved one certain thing she did in bed. Repeat the scene to her.

You don't always have to wait until it is time for sex to talk dirty. For example, there are always times during the day where you could call your partner and make them aroused with a few words. Or you could text her a few times with things like 1) I can't wait to walk through the door so I can go down on you again..."or 2) Does your pussy tickle your legs when you walk? This will have her thinking about the evening to come, and anticipation always heightens the pleasure.

One little trick when talking dirty is to use the word "I" a lot. When you do, it lets the woman know that it is your desire for her to do the thing that she did again. 3) I like it when you... or 4) I want you to.... or 5) I just love it when you... The things you specify are going to stand out in her mind simply by you using the word "I" consistently in your dirty talk. Be sure to use it in a balanced way, though, because you want to know what she wants as well.

When you talk dirty to your partner, it lets her know that you are thinking of her, and desire for her. Women are emotional, and want to know that she is always on your mind. She needs to realize that she is special, and one of the ways to do that is to focus your energy on keeping you on her mind. This way, not only will she slowly be aroused throughout the day, but she will also eventually become more open about trying things with you even, if she did not previously before.

But still, it's important not to put way too much pressure on yourself when it comes to talking dirty. Confidence wins, and if she is kind of shy she'll still follow your lead if you feel comfortable. For example, if you and she were sneaking in a quickie in a place where you could possibly get caught, the thrill and exhilaration would make her want to make love there with you, but as the man you have to remain confident in those moments. It could mean the difference between your erotic episode happening or passing you by.

Chapter 3: Foreplay Tips

Okay, let's get into the tips for foreplay. Among the most requested things that women want guys to do is pay more attention to their boobs. I know, it was a shock to me as well. What guy doesn't just love a nice set of boobs, right? Well, as it turns out, many fellas don't pay enough attention to them during foreplay. It's important to remember that your lady needs to feel sexy herself when slowly building up to sex. That being said, she wants you to play with them more. Take more time to squeeze them and nibble them, and she will definitely appreciate it.

The next thing to remember is to be gentle during foreplay. The way to do this is to simply slow down. You can do what you have planned, but the entire purpose of foreplay is to take your time to be sensual. So, remember to always be soft to the touch. Sometimes guys will be too aggressive with their fingers, for example, around her clit. It turns her on a lot more when you do it slower. Not just finger action either. Everything from kisses to rubs across her body should be done extra slow. It will make your time together that much more special to her if she knows that you are there with her in the moment every step of the way.

Putting on slow music usually helps as well if you have trouble slowing down on your own during foreplay. If she likes smooth jazz you could turn that on for background music, or some sexy R&B. The vibe will change as you play slower music, and you will almost naturally do things like rub and kiss her at a pace that she can really feel. This type of foreplay relaxes her enough so that she can climax when it is time.

One of most complained about things by women as well is also a part of foreplay that should always be followed by guys. Fellas, don't be in such a rush for the end result that you forget to do the one thing that she really wants you to do – undress her. It is a little disappointing to her when she has to take her own clothes off. So again, depending on if she wants rough sex or slow and sensual will determine how aggressively you remove her clothes...just go with the mood.

When you use your tongue during foreplay, it is one of the sexiest things you could do. But, you should not overdo it, whether you are kissing her lips or otherwise. For example, there are not many women who don't absolutely love neck kisses. But although you can use a little tongue here, there is no need to slobber all over it. Too much tongue can be nasty, especially if you are around her ears. A light kiss and lick is okay, but don't make her think that you are trying to clean them for her.

Another mistake women complain about is if we don't use both of our hands during foreplay. For example, if you are going down on her, then you may use both hands for a few minutes in the beginning, but then you will have a free one. The key is to not be lazy. While you are using one hand down low, use the other one to touch her all over her body. Caress her breasts, rub her thighs and her legs. The touch coupled with your clitoral stimulation will make her that much more excited, and the chances of both of you climaxing increases greatly.

Foreplay is about multitasking, if you will. For example, let's say that you are in a missionary position on top and are fingering her. Don't hover over her staring, kiss her simultaneously. She wants you to feel like you are all over her body, and that can be hard to do when you are only focusing on one thing at a time. Multitasking only gets easier and easier as you get to know her better and better, and can even end up leading to new things to try during foreplay. The two of you will continue to evolve as time goes by.

Performing well during foreplay with your lady has a lot to do with doing what you are already supposed to do. How many times have you heard your lady complain about things that have nothing to do with sex, such as you not paying attention to her completely? It's funny, but if you are on the couch with your girl and watching the game and ignoring her, she will likely tell you so many things about yourself that you don't do just to get your attention. Again, one of these things is not noticing when she is trying to do something for you, like wear sexy lingerie.

As men, the minute we see our lady in lingerie we want to commence ripping it off. But, during foreplay, you have to take those moments to take it all in. She put in a lot of time and energy picking it out and couldn't wait to show you how good she looked in it. So, that being said, you need to be prepared to compliment her in some way when she gets up and walks around. Sometimes all you have to do is make sure she sees you staring at her. When she catches you looking, that's when you give her the compliment.

One more thing about foreplay that I have to stress. You need to nibble, not bite. Just as with the tongue too much can be bad, the teeth are the same way! She likes it with a little nibble, not something that will result in teeth marks on her body! Speaking of marks, hold off on the hickies as well. If she likes them, then be sure to do it in inconspicuous places so that the folks at her job the next day don't stare at her during her shift.

Chapter 4: Sexting

Without a section on texting, many of you would be lost, because the majority of communication today is over via messaging. In fact many people text more than they talk with their real voice on the phone. So, that being said, when trying to practice how to talk dirty, texting (or sexting) is in your bag of weapons and tricks. There are certain ones that I will point out that are the most effective, but you are always free to experiment with ones of your own. Some of the ones I mention you will realize that you have used before and didn't even know you were sexting!

It's only right that I start off with one that is so natural that it was popular way before text messages became sext messages. When you inquire about what she has on, it makes her feel as if you are imagining about her right then and there, which you are. When you start off sexting with this line, she will be curious as to what you will say next. You can never go wrong with the sext message 6) What are you wearing? As she begins to describe her clothes to you, it is likely she is already following your lead.

Now, once she gets done with describing what she has on, she will sometimes ask you what you are wearing. Even if she doesn't, you still want to have a back-and-forth dialogue going on, or an in-and-out dialogue, if you will. Describing your clothes to her whether she asks you to or not will let also give you a chance to compliment her, as you should always do when she describes her clothes to you. The exchange of information can be super erotic even in the beginning of the conversation.

Now that you have talked about clothes, the next message you send should hint on something that has nothing to do with clothes – in fact this message will reflect the direct opposite.

You want her to know that you are aroused by her, so you now need to paint a picture in her mind that shows you thinking of her in your private thoughts. You will likely make her smile if you send her a text message telling her that you were thinking of her in the shower that day, or the night before. The shower is intimate, and she'll respond accordingly.

Sexting can also be funny. In fact you will find more funny ones than anything. Being that you are not physically there you want her to have this type of reaction every few messages - a laugh out loud moment. The rest of them should be a little nastier in between the funny ones. A good rotation of messages would be to send two or three private and very sexy ones, then one that is sexy and funny allowing her to laugh every few messages. This way you don't go so deep and keep the sexting fun yet very enticing.

So let's do a quick rotation of sext messages...three very sexy ones and one laugh out loud one. You could start off with 7) You have my heart **and** my pants throbbing right now... Then you could continue with another hot sexy one such as 8) I love your lips...when do I get to see the other set? Then do another one like 9) You turn me on each time you look at me... Then, say something really funny but sexy like 10) I'm texting with this hand but my other one is busy...can you help?

Here are some more fun ones to try on your girl tonight!

11)   You are making me so hard, thinking of your rockin bod.

12) Oh are you wet baby?

13) I wish I had my hands all over you.

14) I can't stop thinking about you.

15) Remember last night, when you went down on me...

16) I want your body now.

17) I want to lick you all over.

18) Let me suck all those juices right out of you.

19) I wanna titty bang you!

20) Let me suck on those nipples.

21) Send me a naughty pic.

22) Oh baby you got my dick begging for it.

23) No one else can make me as hard as you can.

24) Let me see you naked.

25) Do you know what I want to do to you right now?

26) What are you thinking about?

27) Let me please you baby with my lips and nothing else.

28) I want to make you cum so hard.

29) Let me feel you.

30) Oh baby are you getting wet for me?

31) Tell me how much you need me right now.

32) I wanna make love on the beach.

33) You got me losing my focus.

34) I want to eat that ass.

35) I want you to suffocate me with your lips, and not the ones on your face .

36) I wanna finger bang you baby.

37) I am gonna rub your clit so good, you will be begging for me to keep going.

38) I am gonna tease the fuck out of you tonight.

39) I wanna rip off your clothes.

40) Let me fuck you hard.

41) Tell me what you want.

42) Don't be shy baby.

43) I am gonna make you scream.

44) I am gonna choke you with my big dick, but you are going to like it.

45) I am gonna fuck you on the kitchen floor tonight.

46) What kind of panties are you wearing?

47) You wearing that cute little lacy bra right now?

48) I want to rip your clothes off with my teeth.

49) I want to unsnap your bra.

50) Let me love you.

Once you get used to sexting, it will get more and more fun. Sexting is actually a kind of foreplay, being that everything you say can lead up to the ultimate climactic period by the time you actually see one another. Some people say that there is a limit to what you can say on a sext, but depending on how long you have known your partner the phrases you use can have no boundaries. Still, obviously if you just met her you will want to start off with light stuff and gradually work your way up.

Chapter 5: Examples of Dirty Talk

Okay, okay. I know many of you readers are saying to yourself "Enough playing around...can you just give me some stuff to say?!!" I saved this section for last because lots of folks just jump to the things to say and not pay attention to the other important rules of dirty talk in the chapters before. But, if you have paid attention this far you are now ready for the best phrases to use when talking dirty. There are three levels that you need to be able to separate when doing it: the Taming Level, the Dirty Level, and finally the Filthy Level.

The Taming Level is mostly words that you would use to warm up to her. These are the type of phrases that you would use to initiate foreplay. They should always be suggestive in nature, and very flirtatious, but no more than that. You want to tease her with these types of phrases, and make her want you just as much as you want her. Sometimes it may be hard to stay within this territory, but you need to, especially if you just met her. You have to balance your dirty talk adequately.

The second stage is the Dirty Level. This level is in the middle, so you have to be sure to stay in the right zone and not talk too lightly or heavily. At this point you can actually let your hormones take control a little more, and transfer those feelings into words. You will be able to be as open as you need to be to get to that next level, and if you do it right you definitely will. That next level that I am referring to, of course is the last one, the Filthy Level.

Truth be told, many women like to hear the filthy level all the time, then there are others who never want it. When you reach this level, nine times out of ten you have known this woman for a long time, and you and she have already been intimate, probably many times before. This level is for when you want to get really freaky and kinky with your words for her, and many times this dirty talk is used only during sex or immediately before. Either way, if you have made it to this level with her than she is likely going back and forth with you with her own dirty talk already.

What I will do is give examples of each level from the lowest to the highest for the remainder of this chapter. This way you can process the information gradually, and get a feel for the level that you need to take right now with the woman that you like and want to start talking dirty to. If you don't want to say curse words, then you are not going to be able to talk dirty on the highest levels. But, if you don't mind saying a few to get her aroused, then here we go.

The Taming Level

Women love compliments, so you can always start off by telling her how good she smells. Smell is the strongest sense tied to memory, so that's why women are very particular about the scents they wear. She will love it when you notice it. Next you could tell her that you have been thinking about her all day, all week, etc. When she knows that she's been on your mind that long, then she will definitely smile, or respond in a positive fashion.

From there you want to give her compliments about her body...

51)   Oh my God you have a sexy waist...

52)   Damn, girl you have a nice figure...

53)   God broke the mold when he made you.

You want to make her blush at this point, and these are a few body comments that will help you develop more of your own. To go a little further, you could whisper in her ear in a public place...

54)   You know what? I can already taste you on my tongue and lips...

You could use that one if you are about to go down on her as well, but there is something about whispering it to her that makes her panties heat up. You could also use these;

55)   I wanna wrap my arms around you.

56)   You are perfect in every way.

57)   God must have forgot you were an angel.

58)   How can you be so wonderful?

59)   You make me blush just thinking of what I'd do to you.

60)   Girl, you are my everything.

When you compliment her body at this level, how long you have known her will determine what part of her frame you say things about. You would complement her face and clothes if you don't know her that well, but if you are spontaneous and feel comfortable you can tell her...

61)   You have a sexy-shaped ass...

62)   Your legs are so sexy...

Use the word "sexy" a lot, no matter how long you've known her. The keyword in it is "sex", and no matter how gentleman-like you approach her, the goal is still to get her aroused.

63)   Damn, your lips are sexy....

64)   That is one sexy outfit...

65)   It's a crime to be that sexy, girl...

66)   Call the police, this girl is too hot to handle.

67)   You are so beautiful.

68)   Damn you sexy!

69)   That top gives good cleavage.

70)   I love the curves of your body.

71)   Is that shirt new?

72)   I can see your bra through that top honey.

73)   I   wanna   lick   inside   your   panties.

If you are in a relationship you can say

74)   You wanna know something? Tonight you are mine...

That one is good if you live together, so is...

75)   Damn, baby, you have me all turned on...

Make sure she knows that you have had her in mind with

76)   Baby if I told you all of the nasty things I've been thinking about you all day long....

77)   If I told you how long I've waited for you...

78)   I've been thinking of your tits all day long.

79)   Your perfect ass has been on my mind since this morning.

80)   Tonight you do what I say.

81) Let me please you.

82) I've never stopped thinking about you.

83) I've had your taste in my mouth all afternoon...

84) Damn you have me so fucking hard right now....

85) Hold me like you'll never let me go.

86) Give yourself to me.

87) I will satisfy you.

88) I will turn your world upside down.

89) Tonight, it is all about you and me.

90) Let's make some magic.

91) Let me make you happy.

92) I will tell you everything.

93) I want to pleasure you all night long.

As you can see, we are beginning to get into the next level of talk. Make her wet even if she isn't by saying to her

94) Look how wet you are getting...

Even if she has on all of her clothes she will begin to feel it. Use that one at the right moment. Also, use ...

95) I am going to make you scream...

96) I'm gonna have you spelling my name baby...

97) I'm gonna make the neighbors hear you screaming my name...

98) I'm going to make your thighs shiver when you cum...

99)   I am gonna make your lips shake.

100)   Oh you are dripping all over me baby.

101)   I like that feeling baby.

102)   Let me touch you.

103)   I am going to have you fucking like a pro.

104)   Hmm baby, I love the taste of you.

105)   Fuck, I love it when you are wet.

106)   I love the feeling between my fingers.

107)   You smell so good babe.

108)   Look how hard you have me.

Okay, let's move on.

The Dirty Level

Alright. If you have gotten to this point you are in good shape as far as getting her aroused goes. Now all you have to do is use the correct lines to keep it going. The last section was pretty clean being that is was simply for taming. But remember when I said that there would be curse words on the way? Well, from here on out potty-mouth just doesn't describe good enough what you are about to become. Remember, this is not the section to start out with, so if you skipped the other ones go back, right now! ☺

To make it simple, this shit is stuff you will say when you are already hitting the pussy. In fact, you can build from these on your own, she will definitely come back with her own phrases.

109)   Fucking right...take that dick, baby...

When she is letting you go deep inside of her...

110) Damn that shit feels so good....

111) Your pussy is the perfect fit for my dick...

112) Your pussy feels like waterfalls.

113) Bounce on that dick, baby...

114) Damn you one sexy ass bitch...

115) Who is my sexy little bitch?

You can change bitch to "girl", "slut", "thing", or whatever else she may be into.

Go ahead and ask her how she feels as well.

116) Do you like the way I stroke that pussy?

117) Can I go deeper baby?

118) You want it slower or faster?

119) Whose pussy is this?

While you're having sex, you can also ask her...

120) You've been thinking of fucking this dick all day haven't you?

121) I've been hard all day thinking about this good pussy...

Also have fun by saying ....

122) Hell yeah, work that pussy girl!

123) Yes, ride that dick girl!

124) Hell yeah bitch, just like that...

125) Take me to fuck town.

126) Harder baby!

127) Can you feel me in you?

128) I am tearing up that pussy now.

129) Fuck me baby.

130) Rub that ass all over my big cock.

131) I am gonna stuff my cock into your wet pussy.

132) Are you ready for me?

133) Tell me what you like.

The freakier she is will determine if you use "bitch", "slut", "Ho" or whatever, so I want to say here to know what she likes if you take it there. The right dirty word at the right time during sex can make her cum really hard, but you have to be sure to say it at the right time. You need to be sure that she is into being called it, because you don't want to spoil the moment. But, nine times out of ten, if you are at this level then you more than likely have nothing to worry about, and she likes being called those names and more during sex.

134) You are gonna make me fill that pussy up...

135) Oh my God you are gonna make me explode in your pussy...

136) You want to feel it deep inside?

137) You want me to make it rain?

138) I am gonna fill you up good.

139) Let me cum all over you.

140) I wanna cum in you.

141) Taste this cum.

142) You got me about to blow

All of these are good ones for when you are about to cum.

To get her cumming you could say..

143) I want you to splash all over this dick...

144) Gimmie that cream, baby...

145) Cum all over my tongue...

if you are going down on her. Okay, as you can see it is beginning to get really filthy, so let's move on to the last level which is entitled just that.

The Filthy Level

When performing dirty talk (and I use the word "performing" because talking dirty may be out of your original character) the Filthy Level is about as nasty and raunchy as a person can get. There is really no limit to what you can say, and at this point she is enjoying every minute of your words. She is probably going to try to come back with words of her own, and anyone walking past your room is going to catch an earful. That being said, make sure your kids are asleep or away from the house before stepping up your dirty talk to this level, please!

146) You like how I ram that pussy bitch?

147) Say you love this dick...

148) You like daddy's dick don't you?

149) You like my big cock in you?

150) Say you want me to cum.

151) Tell me when you are close to cumming.

152) You like when I take you from behind.

153) Baby scream for me.

154) Oh you have me cumming like a waterfall you little whore.

Also, make sure you say these lines at a nice calm vocal level. These words are strong, and there is no need to scream them, unless of course you can't help it in the moment.

155) You like that don't you, you freaky little slut...

156) You like the way that dick feels in your mouth/pussy, don't you?

157) Say that's my pussy, say that's daddy's pussy...

158) Tell me how much you like that baby.

159) You like that dick in your ass, don't you?

160) I am gonna pound that ass, till I explode.

161) You like it when I slap your ass, don't you?

162) I am gonna slam it in there.

While you are in the middle of sex and she is wailing, you will want her to say some things too. So tell her to say it!

163) Tell me to fuck you harder baby...

164) Tell me to beat that pussy up.

165) Say fuck me daddy.

166) Call me daddy.

167) Tell me to rip that pussy.

168) Tell me you want me to make you scream.

169) Are you gonna swallow for me bitch?

170) Tell me you want me to hurt you.

171) Say my name bitch.

If she is usually quiet in bed, she won't be for long after your specific instructions. You will likely only have to tell her once or twice what you like to hear. After she gets it down she'll become more creative after a few times.

This one has worked wonders. First, tell her to tell you that she hates you. She might say *"What?"* Respond with *"Say it, say I hate you..."* She is going to be at a loss for words, but that's when you hit the pussy really, really hard. Go as deep as and fast as you can! Then ask her again to say it. 172) Tell me you hate me! She'll say *"I hate you!"* Then start back fucking her really hard while saying 173) Okay then, FUCK ME LIKE YOU HATE ME! She is gonna go crazy, dude.

Here are some more fun examples.

172) Just lay back and let me stroke that pussy, baby.

173) I love feeling your tits/ass in my hands...

174) I love the way you taste...

Also, you can use when you climax...

175) I'm gonna cum on your sexy ass...

176) Shake those tits and make daddy cum on them.

177) Daddy is about to cum on those nice lips...

178) You want it on your tongue, here it cums...

179) Here is some milk for those nice titties...

180) I'm gonna cum on that pretty face...

181) Stick out your tongue so I can drip cum on it.

182) Feel this warm cum shoot into your pussy...

183) Let me lick your clit till you cum baby.

184) Tell daddy you like his nice long dick in your tight pussy.

185) Let me see you covered in my cum.

186) Just relax and watch me rip you apart.

187) I'm gonna fuck you so hard, you won't be able to walk tomorrow.

188) Shut your mouth and let me fuck it.

189) Oh honey you got me all hard.

190) I am gonna fuck your tight little pussy bitch!

191) I am gonna make you scream, you little cunt.

192) I am gonna make you speechless.

193) Ohhh fuck you bitch, here I cum.

194) Who is my little whore? You are.

195) Now take this dick.

196) I want you to beg for it.

197) I am gonna fuck you mommy.

198) Turn around so I can shove it up your tight little ass.

199) Let me see those tits!

200) Harder, harder, harder, ..

Have fun.

Talk Dirty:

How to talk to get your man aroused and in the mood for sex!

Introduction

I want to thank you and congratulate you for downloading the book *Talk Dirty*. I wrote this book in hopes that more couples would explore the option of talking dirty in their sexual relationships, as well as to clear up some misconceptions of dirty talk, and to provide just enough information to help make your man's as well as your, sexual fantasies come true.

This book contains proven steps and strategies on how to become a truly confident woman in the ways of talking dirty. With 200 examples of dirty talk, and even a how to section, in which I will lay out the formula for you to create your own dirty talk, this book will become your sexual awakening. Let's face it dirty talk is taking over our world, you hear it in music, you see it in the movies all the time, and more and more people are beginning to use the option of sexting to improve their relationship. Well it is time to wake up and start pleasing your man with those lips of yours, and I am talking about the ones on your mouth. Sheesh get your mind out of the gutter, there will be plenty of that later.

You might think you can't learn to talk dirty, but you can. I will let you in on a little secret, the three key features a woman must have to talk dirty are; confidence, imagination and a sexual appetite. If you have all of these features, then talking dirty is like a walk in the park. Just follow these easy steps and soon you will be creating and acting out your man's every sexual fantasy.

Here's an inescapable fact: you will need confidence and a loving partner. If you want to make your love life stronger, more vibrant, and even a little spontaneous, then don't you dare put down this book. Read all the steps, confidence boosters, and little pick me ups along the way. . . You soon will be talking dirty in your sleep, and just maybe that will be a turn on for your man.

If you do not develop the skills of talking dirty, then please don't give up! Sometimes it takes a little extra time and patience to achieve the confidence and imagination to successfully talk dirty. You will be cumming along in no time ;)

It's time for you to become a confident woman with the capability of talking dirty at the drop of a dime. Next time you see your man, surprise him with a little dirty talk, and maybe he will reciprocate with something more. Don't get stuck into the same old routine, mix it up, go out, have sex on the kitchen floor, go crazy, but most importantly TALK DIRTY.

Chapter 1: Let's Talk About Sex

"Let's talk about sex baby. Let's talk about you and me. Let's talk about all the good things and the bad things that may be. Let's talk about sex. Let's Talk about Sex." -Salt N'Pepa

Why is it so difficult for some couples to talk about sex? I mean cum on! Sex is a healthy part of life, and should be enjoyed. Why are we still cowering in the corner every time it is mentioned? Why do we feel it is this disgusting action, and why are there so many misconceptions and arguments over it? Why? There doesn't need to be. It's time to talk about it.

Communicate to your man, tell him what you like and what you don't like. Don't assume he will know what to do if you don't tell him. I am sure he has no problem telling you what he likes and if he isn't speaking up, then let this be a lesson to you both. COMMUNICATE!

Sex isn't just for love, but it is also for pleasure. If you aren't doing it as much, or you no longer feel attracted to one another, then fix it. Make time, take time out of your day to tell your man how much he means to you. Try something new, don't get stuck in the same routine, and open yourself up to other possibilities. The possibilities are endless if you allow yourself to be sexually awakened.

Try something different, allow yourself to use your imagination and talk dirty. It is important for couples to talk dirty to one another once in a while, it keeps things fresh and exciting. I know many of you are thinking , only hookers and slutty girls talk to their man that way, but newsflash this is the 21st century if you want to sext your man during your lunch break, then go right ahead or if you want to text him a dirty little message late at night, then what is stopping you?

Talking dirty is becoming more and more popular as time goes on. It seems there are even more ways to talk dirty than before. You could use your phone, laptop, tablet, Facebook to IM him, or the good old fashion, face to face technique.

Here are some favorites of mine that are sure to get you on his mind. There will be 200 examples throughout the book, so keep a look out as the numbers increase ;)

1. I want you so bad.

2. I'm so wet thinking of your rock hard long throbbing cock.

3. Oh I wish you were here so you could pound my little pussy.

4. I love it when you make me scream.

5. I want you to lick me all over.

6. I want to do so many bad things to you.

7. I wanna suck you like a lollipop.

8. Let's fuck in public.

9. (()) D====8

10. Tell me how bad you want it.

11. Tell me what you want to do to me.

12. Bend me over and use that pole.

13. Slam it in, I wanna scream.

14. Slap my ass, and pull my hair.

15. I want you to cum all over my face and tits.

16. I want to swallow your delicious cum.

17. I want you to fuck me till I can't walk anymore.

18. I need you now.

19. I miss you so bad, come here and give me a taste.

20. Just the tip.

21. Hold me down, and show me what you got.

22. I want you to choke me with that big cock of yours

23. I want to be gasping for breath, as I suck you off, and go deeper and deeper.

24. Oh I want you to make me cum.

25. I'm about to cum, I'm so close, oh right there yeah.

26. Lick me all over.

27. Lick my tits.

28. Get naked.

29. I've been thinking about you.

30. You were in my dreams last night.

31. Fuck me

32. Don't stop

33. 8====D

34. Faster

35. I'm almost there

Those are just a few, but you catch my drift.

Chapter 2: Awkward Turtle
How to not be awkward when talking dirty...

Talking dirty is a skill, so it might take lots of time to perfect it. In the beginning you will most likely feel awkward, turn red, blush or even giggle. You need to be able to get that awkwardness and laughing sensation out of your system.

So how do you get that awkwardness and push it aside, so you can finally awaken? My first suggestion is to be naked. Seems like a silly suggestion, but studies show being naked more helps you appreciate your body and become more comfortable in your skin. After a long day of work, just go upstairs, strip down, look at yourself in a mirror and say "I am a confident, beautiful woman, who will show her man a whole new side of her." Do this 3 times a week, or every day if you want. Do it for as long as you need.

If being naked isn't something you want to try, then maybe communicate to your man. Explain how you are trying something different, and to keep an open mind. Tell him that you are going to rock his world. Men always love hearing that.

To get rid of possible giggles, watch a horror movie right before you are about to talk dirty, or get yourself in a real serious manner. Honestly, I think the laughing, and the awkwardness is all related to lack of self-worth and confidence. I know you have all heard of the saying "You need to love yourself first before you can love anyone." This rings true to talking dirty. How can you feel comfortable saying such vulgar things, when you aren't even comfortable with yourself?

Make sure you are comfortable, confident and imaginative when you begin. I will be having a chapter on What Not to Do with Dirty Talk, but that will be closer to the end of the book. I will give you a sneak peek here though...

Whatever you do, don't say something that offends you or your man. Turning your man on does not have to be degrading. You know what I mean, don't let him do things that you aren't comfortable with or upsets you. If talking dirty brings out a side of him you have never seen, make sure you lay down boundaries.

One woman I spoke with told me her boyfriend got so into the dirty talk that instead of having vaginal sex, he did anal and didn't let her know. Imagine that surprise! Ouch! Needless to say that night didn't end well, and it makes sense why. She wasn't comfortable with that type of sex, and maybe even told her boyfriend she never wanted to do anal, but it happened. Just imagine that night. So remember always say things you mean and intend to do, so you can avoid the above scenario.

I bet he was feeling like an awkward turtle. Don't let your dirty talk become awkward, keep it simple, sexy, and creative.

Chapter 3: Start Your Engines

Dirty Conversation Starters

Isn't it strange how the older men get the more difficult it is to start them up? Seriously, in high school, all over you, college, a fuckfest for sure, but marriage, not a lot of sexual activity on the radar. Plus you've seen the commercial for erectile dysfunction, how could you not? I swear they run that commercial into the ground. Doesn't matter what I am doing, eating dinner, cleaning, or writing, there it is that commercial. A commercial that has forever stained the male ego.

So how can you get your man in the mood? Now, I mean in the mood for anything; dirty talk, sex, or foreplay. How? I ask you, how.

One fun strategy is to use penis shaped food. There are plenty of options, and look bananas are even considered an aphrodisiac! Or what about a nice long hot dog, that you can put in and out of your mouth. A Popsicle even, a spoon, a straw, etc. The possibilities are endless.

With your imagination and creativity you can make anything sexual. You can start to get your man thinking about sex and dirty talk with just a lick of your lips. The real secret is, you have the power. You can make your man hang on to your every word, make him jump at the chance to have sex with you, make him start to talk dirty more and more often. Never forget that. The power is in your hands,

So next time you are at the mall with your man, if you are feeling pretty spontaneous, take the straw from your drink and suck it up and down. Not only will this action surprise your man, but it might make him reciprocate in words. Obviously he can't just take you in the food court, but you will definitely be on his mind. Being on his mind is the first way to start his arousal, the rest is up to him!

Chapter 4: Sexting Tips

How to talk dirty like a pro

This is the moment you have all been waiting for! This part of the book is the how to section in which I will give detailed instructions on how to talk dirty. I will give you a formula so to speak, and we will go from there.

First, you need to figure out how comfortable you are with what you are about to be saying. More simply put-know your limits. Do not say something if you have no desire to follow up with it. Do not say something if it offends you or him, or could be seen as degrading.

Second, know the environment you or your man are in. If you know he is at work, don't be sending dirty pics or dirty talk his way. His boss might see it, or he might get in trouble. If you know his lunch break schedule, then send it then. With all of these technological complications present, it is no wonder why most people do it the old fashion way of face to face. However, this chapter focuses on the technological aspects of talking dirty, so let's proceed.

Now dirty talk usually begins with a phrase, short, small and to the point. Maybe when you become more skilled, you can get more detailed, but for now we will stick to a few words.

Here is the formula: Begin with the word "your" then move to an adjective, then move to the body part, and end with an action. This is just a beginning exercise. 36) **Your throbbing cock makes me so wet**. You can change the formula up for instance instead of using the word "your" you could just say "I want" or "I need." So it could go like this 37) **I want your hard penis in me**.

You could also just say a few words to get your point across such as, 38) make me cum, 39) harder, 40) I'm so wet, 41) fuck me, 42)I want it now, etc.

Most importantly you should use your imagination. Using your imagination could make talking dirty more spontaneous and pleasurable. Use the same formula, but change it up. Maybe use more adjectives, or use a fun word to describe the body part. Here are some examples; 43) throbbing pole, 44) pitch that tent in my backyard, 45) snake, 46) the dicktator, 47) fuck puppet, 48) dong, 49) sperminator, 50) tonsil tickler, etc. Go wild.

Here are some more great examples:

51. I love your ass in those jeans.

52. You make me wanna cum just looking at you.

53. You have the most amazing cock I have seen.

54. God I must have you now.

55. Rub my clit with your hard cock.

56. Your cock is stretching me out.

57. I want to feel every inch of your cock in me.

58. I want you to fill my pussy with that cum of yours.

59. Let me suck that cock, before you put it back in me.

60.   Slap my ass harder

61. Finish on my ass.

62. Go slowly, I want to enjoy this.

63. Come make my pussy wet.

64. Shove that big cock in my ass.

65. I'm going to fuck you so hard.

66. Do you want to cum on me baby?

67. Do you want to fill my pussy with cum?

68. You are filling me all up baby.

69. Oh don't stop, not yet.

70. I want to make you moan and scream.

71. Say my name.

72. I've been very naughty, punish me.

73. That incredible, Fuck me again.

74. Tease me with your big throbbing cock.

75. Tell me how much you love it.

76. No one has even turned me on as much as you have.

77. Your body is so hot.

78. You are so sweaty.

79. Your penis drives me wild.

80. I want to ride you right now, so hard.

81. Let me get on top.

82. Let me rock your world.

83. Let me take the lead.

84. Do you want to punish me?

85. Do you want to make me scream?

86. Use those handcuffs on me

87. Cover my eyes, and get freaky.

88. Say my name when you do that.

89. I want to get naked with you right now.

90.   Kiss me down under.

91. Do you like when I do that?

92. Do you like how that feels?

93. I love the things you do with your tongue.

94. I'm going to control you tonight.

95. I am going to make you my slave tonight.

96. You are the best lover I have ever had.

97. Show me what you can do.

98. Shut my mouth up with that big cock of yours.

99. Just lie back and let me make you cum,

100.   You taste so good.

Sexting makes you feel more vulnerable, because you won't be able to see his reaction, but you will know he is thinking about you. Another thing is sexting is a less effective way of dirty talk. He can't hear how you are saying it, your tone, the speed, or even if you are doing actions as well.

Sexting is a fun sexy way to remind your man you are thinking about him. A little dirty text, he will be thinking about you all day long and wondering what you are up to. You will become his little mystery. So when you are talking dirty to your man, remember less is more.

Chapter 5: Foreplay Tips
Make it last...

I know a lot of women complain that men are never interested in foreplay. Men always go right to it, nothing more and nothing less. If only men knew how much they were missing out on, if they tried a little foreplay.

Foreplay does a lot more than you think, and is actually very similar to dirty talk. Both are little pick me ups and helpful ways to create sexual tension in the relationship. Foreplay also gives you more time, more options and in the long run makes it last. So guys why wouldn't you try foreplay?

There are several options for foreplay.

You could dress up, be different people for the night, or act out certain scenarios. Your man could be a convict, and you could be his hostage. Or simple ones like pretending to have an affair. Some people don't like going too extreme when it comes to foreplay, so I have a few more options for you.

Take time appreciating each other's' bodies. Caress his arms, penis, and slowly lick his shaft up and down. Don't neglect the balls. If anything the balls should be the main star when it comes to foreplay, because they are often neglected during intercourse. Cradle his balls, suck each one in your mouth, nibble a little, and don't forget to stroke. While you are caressing the balls, go towards the shaft and go up and down with your tongue.

Another option is to make the dirty talk a form of foreplay. For this to work you really need to work on your delivery. You need to focus on your tone, body language, and speed of delivery. You could say it really slowly, and take dramatic pauses. You could whisper it or say it in a raspy voice. While talking always caress either his shoulder, arms or hands. Make sure you are doing an action other than speaking when you are talking dirty. Don't talk too fast, slow the speed down, almost as if you are done talking but then start again. This keeps him on his feet and guessing. Make sure you are keeping eye contact for a little, but then look away to tease him and keep it playful. One thing to remember when talking dirty is to always keep it playful and fun, never too serious or too demanding.

Next time your man wants to jump right into the sack, suggest foreplay, or further more just whisper in his ears these words 101) "I want you now." You could say something else as well, this is just to get you started.

Here are some more examples to use:

102. You make me so horny, baby.

103. I love it when you nibble on my nipples.

104. Don't you dare cum, until I tell you that you can.

105. Lick every inch of me.

106. I love how fast your cock can get hard.

107. Your wish is my command.

108. Don't stop, till I tell you to.

109. Do that some more.

110. I am going to lick and suck you till you come.

111. I want to have those lips all over me.

112. Fuck me naughty boy.

113. You can have me anyway you want.

114. Keep touching me down there.

115. Finger me till I squirt

116.   I love when you go down on me.

117.   I love how you use your tongue

118.   Use your mouth on me.

119.   Don't tell me to stop.

120.   I want to kiss you all over.

121.   Get that cock ready for me.

122.   Hold me down and cum all over.

123.   You are so sexy.

124.   You got me dripping wet.

125.   You have me thinking of you every minute of the day.

126.   You make me so weak.

127.   You make me want to lick every part of you.

128.   I want to suck those balls.

129.   I want to feel those balls pounding my pussy.

130.   Kiss me harder.

131.   I love feeling your strong arms.

132.   I love how you smell.

133.   I love the taste of you.

134.   I love your cum.

135.   I love you so much.

136.   Tell me you want it.

137.   Tell me you like this.

138.   Tell me you love me.

139.   Why can't you see how wet you get me?

140.   Keep fingering me, don't stop.

141.   Don't forget my ass.

142.   Keep pounding me.

143.   I want to make you cum.

144.   I want to exhaust you.

145.   Never forget I made you feel that way.

146.   I've never cum so hard.

147.   I've never felt so wet.

148.   I've never had such an orgasm.

149.   Oh fuck, fuck me good

150.   Use that tongue of yours.

151.   Harder, faster, cum for me.

152.   Keep doing that, I like it

153.   Use that tongue like you mean it.

154.   Keep me wet

155.   Be forceful with me

156.   Make me blush

157.   Take me to fucktown

158.   Only you can make me feel this way

159.   Your cock feels so good in my hands.

160.   I never want you to stop.

161.   Let me take control

162.   Oh you like putting that up my ass, huh?

163. You are gonna make me a cum pie.

164. Can I just worship you?

165. I want to play with your balls.

166. Tell me how bad you want me

167. Oh you have me soaking wet, come in me and play

168. Be my little secret.

169. Make me cum in every room.

170. You got me wishing I knew you earlier.

171. Choke me with that cock of yours

172. I'm gagging on you, please don't stop.

173. You are big as fuck.

174. You like that big boy?

175. Tell me just how much you want me

176. Kiss me like you mean it

177. You take my breath away

178. Explore my caverns

179. Use your sperminator on me.

180. Use that dick of yours

181. I love it when I get you hard.

182. You are so hot.

183. Your muscles are bulging

184. I want that dick in me now

185. Your penis makes me wet.

186. Tell me why you gotta be so good....

187.   Don't tell me to stop screaming, I like it.

188.   Oh oh oh fuck that feels good.

189.   Cum for me baby

Chapter 6: Say What?!
What not to do with dirty talk . . .

So we have gone through why dirty talk is so important, many examples, the formula for it and even some helpful hints. However, one thing we really need to clarify is what not to do with dirty talk.

Dirty talk is a new focus to explore, but with every exploration you need to be careful. As already addressed earlier on, make sure what you say you follow up with. Nothing is worse than getting a guy excited, and then ending up with blue balls. Make sure what you say doesn't offend or bring up some kind of drama. Possibly what you say could be degrading to you, or even offend your man. Make sure you are comfortable with what you are saying. If you are not comfortable with what you are saying then don't say it. If you don't mean it, then what is the point? Just make sure to continue working on becoming more and more confidence. With confidence your dirty talking ability will really improve.

Another thing you want to make sure is that you dirty talk in appropriate environments. This was already discussed earlier on in the book, but should be repeated. Someone could lose their job if done in the wrong environment. You wouldn't want your man's boss reading a text you sent for his eyes only, and vice versa.

Another thing to keep in mind is talking dirty is a fun, and a flirty way of creating sexual tension. However, if you are always talking dirty, this won't be a surprise for your man anymore, so it will lose its appeal if you will. So you need to make sure that when you are talking dirty that you don't overdo it. If you keep doing it, then your man will begin to expect it, and then you will fall into the same old routine.

Don't laugh, or be awkward with your dirty talk. This will most certainly ruin the mood, and then you will be screwed-not in the good way. Don't say over complicated phrases, the point of dirty talk is to be short and to the point. No one wants to read a paragraph of porn, but a flirty little text like 190) "You make me so wet" with a winky face, now that kills every time.

Last but not least, make sure you have fun with it.

Conclusion

Thank you again for downloading this book!

I hope this book was able to help you successfully learn to dirty talk, and help arouse your man. I hope this book has made you feel more confident and comfortable in your abilities. I wanted this book to shed some light on the concept of dirty talk and be able to help with your relationship. Hopefully you have learned a few tricks, and are eager to please your man tonight! Don't forget the formula, and add your own flavor to it. Get creative, imagine no one else is in the room but you and him.

The next step is to experiment. Try out the formula, try out the tips, spice up your love life and make the next time you have sex an unforgettable experience. Use some of the examples on your man the next time you see him, and see his reaction. Always communicate no matter how awkward you might feel, you must be open and allow yourself to be sexually awakened.

With every awakening, it only takes one thing, or one time to be fully open to the possibilities. So give yourself to sex, spread those legs and let him in.

I'll end with a few more creative examples of dirty talk found in movies.

191.   "Take me to bed or lose me forever" (TopGun)

192.   "I want you inside of me" (Ghostbusters)

193.   " I wanna be on you" (Anchorman)

194.   "I'm glad he's single because I'm going to climb that like a tree" (Bridesmaids).

195.   "When was the last time you came so hard and so long you forgot where you are?" (Torchwood)

196.   "How would you like to have a sexual encounter so intense it could conceivably change your political views?"(The Sure Thing)

197.   "I don't make love. I fuck. Hard. (Fifty Shades of Grey)

198.   "One day, lady superspy Susan Cooper, I will fuck you (Spy)

199.   "Do I make you horny, baby?" (Austin Powers: International Man of Mystery)

200.   "You must forgive my lips....they find pleasure in the most unusual places."(A Good Year)

Finally, if you enjoyed this book, please take the time to share your thoughts and post a review on Amazon. It'd be greatly appreciated!

Thank you and good luck!

Sexting Tips for Women:

100 tips to turn him on!

Introduction

I want to thank you and congratulate you for downloading the book *Sexting Tips for Women*. I wrote this book in hopes that more couples would explore the option of sexting and dirty talk in their sexual relationships, as well as to clear up some misconceptions of dirty talk, and to provide just enough information to help make your man's as well as your, sexual fantasies come true.

This book contains proven steps and strategies on how to become a truly confident woman in the ways of talking dirty and sexting. It is time to wake up and start pleasing your man with those lips of yours, and I am talking about the ones on your mouth. Sheesh get your mind out of the gutter, there will be plenty of that later.

Here is a synopsis of what you will learn:

-Why foreplay is important to sex
-How to tease your man
-How to sext and how not to sext
-100 less naughty sexting tips
-100 much more naughty sexting tips

Chapter 1: Why foreplay is necessary (and downright sexy…)

For a massive ejaculation for your man and a massive orgasm for you-foreplay is a must! For women, it takes women a longer time to build up the necessary levels of arousal. Therefore, a slower and steady build up to orgasm is necessary. Foreplay prepares the body and mind for sex and makes the two of you hornier than if you simply walked right into sex.

Letting your man get in your pussy too easy is not good for orgasm. Do not rush through foreplay. Just like a runner needs to do a 10-15 minute warm-up before a long run-a couple needs to sexually tease each other and build up anticipation before a sex session.

Studies have shown that women need around 20 minutes of arousal time to reach the "orgasmic platform." Skipping the sex-response cycle makes it hard for men to ejaculate and cum and for women to orgasm. In the case of sex, patience pays!

You need to tell your man that foreplay is a must. Horny texts or sayings build sexual tensions. Both are little pick me ups and helpful ways to create sexual tension in the relationship. Foreplay also gives you more time, more options and in the long run makes it last. So guys why wouldn't you try foreplay?

Here are some basic foreplay tips:

Dirty Talk: I wrote two other books on this-but to summarize-men love women who do dirty talk. It is a huge turn on. Phrases such as "Pound my little wet pussy", "I want to lick, fuck, and suck your juicy sticky hard throbbing cock", "Bite my tits", or "I'm going to sit on your face and rub my wet pussy in your face" are huge turn-ons and great for foreplay.

Roleplay: I have an upcoming book on naughty sex-but to summarize exploring different roleplaying is a huge turn on. Dressing up like a slutty secretary or a sexy teacher is an awesome foreplay method.

Teasing: Gradually build up. You don't want to be giving head to a limp penis. Instead, as I always say-incorporate some foreplay first. Several minutes of groping, hand playing and making out are a great way to start. You can also kiss and lick his inner thighs several inches from his penis. This area is very sensitive and is a huge turn on.

Whisper something dirty in his ear: Tell him "I want your cock now!" real quietly in his ear.

Fondling: For no reason, grab his load or slap his butt. And don't ask for permission.

Chapter 2: How to tease your man sexually:

Playing a little hard to get along with some teasing is huge to success in the bedroom.

Here are some basic tips on teasing your man:

Attack him by surprise: An unexpected hug from behind or kiss will warm him up. Come up behind him, hug him, and then kiss the back of his neck. Squeezing his butt or slipping your hand down his crotch and graze against his cock will drive him nuts.

Make him work for it: In the middle of a make out session, put your hand on his chest and push him away moderately aggressively. Then move to the other end of the bed and say "come and get me."

Public Displays of Affection: Hold your man's hand while you two are walking. When sitting, have your hand on his thighs. If the moment is right, graze your hand over his package.

Touch: Some great places to touch your man are his forearms, his shoulders, thighs, lower back, and face.

Be naked more often: Being naked for no reason in your home or apartment is hot to your man.

Wear lingerie: Bending over near his face while you are wearing sexy slutty lingerie is hot. Pretend that you don't know that he is watching!

Play hard to get: Instead of simply saying "lets have sex tonight", say " I hope you behave well tonight!" or "I'm not sure if I'm going to spend the night tonight." Humans have a tendency to want what we can't have, which is why this builds attraction.

Compliment him sexually: Even telling him simply he looks strong, he's smart, funny, sexy, etc. are all still turn ons.

Wink at him: His mind will start to wonder what dirty thoughts you are thinking!

Brush against him: When walking by, "accidently" brush your hand past his butt. Or, if he is sitting on the couch, lean over and give him a kiss. "Accidentally" brush your boobs against his arm.

Release it: Too much teasing is a bad thing. Teasing without releasing is constant foreplay without and end goal. This will leave your man frustrated and impatient. Tease a little, then back off. Tease a little, then back off again.

Leave hints around him about sex: leaving a sex toy out in the open, or eating penis shaped food, or leaving some of your panties on the floor is great for this.

Chapter 3: Sexting 101

Sharing intimate information or showing some skin over the phone has become common and more risky these days. Approximately 32% of men and 38% of women regularly sext. That's a lot of naughty photos and messages being sent around the world! Sending steamy texts to your partner, if done right, can be a great relationship booster. Many people are more turned on by written words over phone and written erotica then they are by porn. Hence, you need to know how to do it right.

Here are your Sexting 101 tips:

Use sexting as foreplay: Sending your man a naughty message while you're at work is a great way to get him out of his head at the corporate grind and get excited to be home. Keep the texts short-but also keep them detailed, juicy, and graphic.

Be Kinky: When you remove all unnecessary barriers in sex communication-everything gets better. Couples who are open and horny in regards to their sexual desires have much more satisfaction in their relationships then couples who don't. Don't be afraid to be dirty with your partner! Life is too short to be perfect. Use a combination of playful talk ("I'm infatuated with how soft your lips are") and more raunchy, pornographic talk (i.e. "I want to swallow your hard cock," or "I want your tongue up my pussy").

Be careful about pictures: If you want to send your man any naughty pictures-you have to be careful. Due to the social media prevalence these days-you don't want that leaking out! However, if you send him any nude pics, make sure you don't show your face or anything that can reveal your identity and that the pic goes no higher than your boobs. You don't want your face on a nude body over the internet! With this precaution-if something leaks-at least no one will be able to tie a face to it.

If your man chooses to send you dickpics (which most women agree is not sexy), that's fine. However-make sure he understands that his face shouldn't be visible either.

Use a password on your phone: You do not want someone else's eyes on your steamy texts! Taking this precaution along with never leaving your phone unattended will eliminate the chance of someone else seeing anything.

Start out slow: do not get raunchy too quickly! This communicates to your man that you are too easy. Be playful and teasing at first. Once you've gotten to know your man for a longer period of time-then you can get to the more r-rated and x-rated texting.

Bring back a memory of his: This doesn't apply if the two of you haven't had sex yet. However, if the two of you had a horny experience that really turned both of you on-text him about it! For example "remember that time that you exploded cum in my mouth for 45 seconds? I can't handle myself. That was so hot." This will make him think back and want to repeat the past!

Ask him a dirty question: Asking him something to get him thinking of dirty things between the two of you is a huge turn on. For example "What would you do to me if I was wearing nothing but a trenchcoat at the front door?" spikes curiosity and fantasies in his head.

Compliment him: Men love being told how awesome they are. Tell him something like "you are making me so wet". Even something more PG works. Telling him you think he's hot and sexy is often enough too.

Do a sext strip tease: Show your man a picture of you fully clothed. Then send another with your bra and panties. Then remove the bra. Then the panties. However, remember to not show your face!!!

Sext him about your fantasies: If you aren't confident enough to tell your man in person about your fantasies-sext your man about them! Whether it be bdsm, threesomes, getting gangbanged, etc. I have a book titled "Spice up your sex life!" about this!

Chapter 4: Sexting Don'ts

Now that we've discussed how to sext-its just as important to figure out exactly how not to do it.

No childish talk: Don't say anything childish like "pee-pee" or "wee-wee." Use adult words. Cock would suffice much better. Get comfortable with using words like cock, pussy, tits, fuck, etc.

Don't do it too soon: Make sure you give yourself some time before you sext with someone. Many women have the habit of getting into it too soon. This communicates that it is too easy to get in your pants. Get to know your man's integrity first.

If you send a picture of your vagina to a man you barely know-you are in for a world of hurt. Too many leaks happen and don't think that it won't happen to you.

Don't store the photos on your phone: Save the photos elsewhere.

Don't sext the wrong person: Double check the phone number before you send the text message. You don't want your mom or dad to get a photo of your naked ass! That would make holiday dinners awkward.

Don't sext while drunk: You are very likely to make a sext that you will regret if you sext while drunk. You will likely sext the wrong person, too many people, or even post on social media. Definitely do not do this!

Do not wait too long to respond to a sext: Waiting too long kills the arousal. If your man sexts you but you don't sext back for 10 hours-chances are he will get busy with something else. He will likely not be aroused all day waiting to reply to your text.

Don't use emoticons: Emoticons are childish and take away the sex appeal. If they come up with blowjob, pussylicking, or anal sex emoticons-fine. However, for the most part you need to be mindful that for the most part these are childish and make the dirty talk less sexy.

Chapter 5: Sexting Examples (less naughty)

Now that we've given you some tips on how to and not sext-let's see how it is done in practice.

It is important that we distinguish between the less naughty and the more naughty texts.

Right below are some great sexts you can send your man to turn him on:

1. What are you wearing right now?

2. Are you alone tonight? Want to play a game?

3. I was thinking about you in the shower today.

4. I will see you in a while. I have got a sexy surprise for you.

5. I am wearing all red today, even the stuff underneath my dress.

6. What do you want me to wear later tonight?

7. Let's tease.

8. You and me, in the back of my car tonight?

9. When you are around, everything starts throbbing and it is not just my heart I am talking about.

10. I think your lips are really sensuous. I am talking about the ones I can see, you still have to show me the other one.

11. If you are tired then I can give you a massage tonight. Let me know where you want my hands to work the most.

12. Want to scream tonight? Stop by my place for a little while.

13. I sometimes feel like playing with your beautiful hair... and other things too.

14. You know how to push the right buttons.

15. Next time we see each other, I am going to show you what love is.

16. I do not need to watch porn anymore. One look at your sexy body keeps me going.

17. Why are your keeping me starved?

18. Next time when I am around you, wear something that keeps me guessing.

19. I want to take you to a place called orgasmland.

20. Want to see my '50 Shades of Grey'?

21. I am feeling very restless. Would you please come by and tie me up tonight? I will let you do whatever you want to do with me.

22. I want to force a few things on you tonight. Permission to be rough?

23. I will be your prisoner tonight.

24. Can I have my way with you?

25. If you could read my mind, you would start feeling really shy around me.

26. How can you turn me on so much just by looking at me?

27. What are your plans with me later tonight? Want to eat something delicious?

28. The next time you pass me by, I am going to tap it.

29. Your wardrobe needs to be updated. How about trying me on?

30. Let me be a part of your favorite fantasy?

31. I had a dream of you last night; you were mostly naked in it.

32. I can probably reach climax just by staring at your behind.

33. I got a whole new way to love you. Want to know what?

34. I feel like having some peaches and cream tonight, with you.

35. How about chocolate syrup all over?

36. What were you thinking yesterday when your hands were all over me?

37. I want to be naughty with you in the office.

38. Are your folks home tonight? I hope not. I do not want them to hear you screaming.

39. I have got a BIG surprise for you. It is in my pants and it will BLOW your mind.

40. Thanks to your skinny jeans, I already know how your behind would feel like.

41. I feel wasted just by looking at your pictures.

42. It gives me goose bumps just by thinking what will I do to your body.

43. Are you ready to go all night?

44. Did you tell me to 'come and get it' with your eyes last night?

45. Would you be my prey and I will be your hunter?

46. Would you like me to take you under?

47. My favorite thing on a dessert is whipped cream. Would you let me put it on you?

48. I know what you want and I think I am ready.

49. I got a plan for the both of us, but it involves my bed in it as well.

50. Just to let you know, I am a rider.

51. I have read some sexy things on the internet. Would you let me try it on you?

52. Why am I horny and you are so far away?

53. I think I need a doctor for this little love disease that I got. Would you please examine me from top to bottom?

54. I have got a new move. Will you let me show it to you later?

55. I have heard that you should not fight it, if you like it.

56. You left me turned on last night. Can you either switch it off or take it a bit further?

57. I really like your tie. Let us use it tonight.

58. Can you please save some energy for later, after you finish your gym? I have got a task for you.

59. I will let you frisk me if you will come and see me in next half an hour.

60. I will let you see mine if I will get to see yours.

61. Want to play tonight?

62. I have been thinking about some seriously racy stuff about you today.

63. You can look at it but you cannot touch it, YET.

64. Let us skip dinner tonight and eat something else.

65. We should stay in a hotel tonight. I am not sure if my neighbors would appreciate all the pounding noise and screaming.

66. I will follow you everywhere, as long as you will let me COME with you.

67. You have got a hypnotic cleavage. I do not think I can look at anything else but it, when we are together.

68. Your bulge is driving me mad.

69. Your dessert is HOT and READY for you.

70. Do you know if there is a way that I can resist those juicy lips of yours?

71. Why cannot I take your wet kisses out of my mind?

72. How will I be able to contain myself when I know that you are in the shower right now?

73. Did you think about me when you were in the bath tub today?

74. Just the smell of you gives me shivers.

75. I just looked at your picture on my phone and darling, you have sent my dial on high.

76. Let's get dirty tonight and wash it off each other in the shower later.

77. I am so much into you. I want to be in you.

78. I am thirsty, when can I see you?

79. I just want to feel your weight on me.

80. Would you let me ride you again?

81. Would you send me some pictures? Pictures you have not sent to anybody else.

82. Tonight in the club we will have our own dancing session, in a dark corner.

83. I have lost something. Would you let me look for it in your pants?

84. How about I come by to your office and you give me a tour of your insides?

85. I will pick you up by 8 o'clock tonight. Wear a skirt or a dress; my hands are a bit restless today.

86. It is really hot today, I think I am going to take my all my clothes off and just lay in my bed. See you in ten?

87. I have a JOB opportunity for you. Interested?

88. I was cooking something with lots of strawberries in it. I am covered in it now, would you come and lick it off me?

89. I am craving for you.

90. You are so kind to me. I am thinking of pleasing you all night tonight.

91. I am sending you this text with one hand, my other hand is busy. Come and join me.

92. You are going to be really exhausted by the end of the night tonight.

93. I want to serve you.

94. I want to kiss you so bad… all over.

95. I want to feel your strong grip on me.

96. All we are going to do tonight is teasing. Are you ready for the torture?

97. I am tired of sending you texts or speaking on phone. Why do not you come here and sit on the top of me?

98. How did you feel when I groped you in a public place last night... in my dream?

99. I am dripping with love and desire for you.

100. Come on and soak me dry with that mouth of yours.

Chapter 6: Sexting Examples (very naughty)

Do not be afraid to use these. Be a brave, hot sexy woman and turn him on!

1. I love your ass in those jeans.
2. You make me wanna cum just looking at you.
3. You have the most amazing cock I have seen.
4. God I must have you now.
5. Rub my clit with your hard cock.
6. Your cock is stretching me out.
7. I want to feel every inch of your cock in me.
8. I want you to fill my pussy with that cum of yours.
9. Let me suck that cock, before you put it back in me.
10. Slap my ass harder
11. Finish on my ass.
12. Go slowly, I want to enjoy this.
13. Come make my pussy wet.
14. Shove that big cock in my ass.
15. I'm going to fuck you so hard.
16. Do you want to cum on me baby?
17. Do you want to fill my pussy with cum?
18. You are filling me all up baby.
19. Oh don't stop, not yet.

20. I want to make you moan and scream.

21. Say my name.

22. I've been very naughty, punish me.

23. That incredible, Fuck me again.

24. Tease me with your big throbbing cock.

25. Tell me how much you love it.

26. No one has even turned me on as much as you have.

27. Your body is so hot.

28. You are so sweaty.

29. Your penis drives me wild.

30. I want to ride you right now, so hard.

31. Let me get on top.

32. Let me rock your world.

33. Let me take the lead.

34. Do you want to punish me?

35. Do you want to make me scream?

36. Use those handcuffs on me

37. Cover my eyes, and get freaky.

38. Say my name when you do that.

39. I want to get naked with you right now.

40. Kiss me down under.

41. Do you like when I do that?

42. Do you like how that feels?

43. I love the things you do with your tongue.

44. I'm going to control you tonight.

45. I am going to make you my slave tonight.

46. You are the best lover I have ever had.

47. Show me what you can do.

48. Shut my mouth up with that big cock of yours.

49. Just lie back and let me make you cum,

50. You taste so good.

51. I want you so bad.

52. I'm so wet thinking of your rock hard long throbbing cock.

53. Oh I wish you were here so you could pound my little pussy.

54. I love it when you make me scream.

55. I want you to lick me all over.

56. I want to do so many bad things to you.

57. I wanna suck you like a lollipop.

58. Let's fuck in public.

59. (()) D====8

60. Tell me how bad you want it.

61. Tell me what you want to do to me.

62. Bend me over and use that pole.

63. Slam it in, I wanna scream.

64. Slap my ass, and pull my hair.

65. I want you to cum all over my face and tits.

66. I want to swallow your delicious cum.

67. I want you to fuck me till I can't walk anymore.

68. I need you now.

69. I miss you so bad, come here and give me a taste.

70. Just the tip.

71. Hold me down, and show me what you got.

72. I want you to choke me with that big cock of yours

73. I want to be gasping for breath, as I suck you off, and go deeper and deeper.

74. Oh I want you to make me cum.

75. I'm about to cum, I'm so close, oh right there yeah.

76. Lick me all over.

77. Lick my tits.

78. Get naked.

79. I've been thinking about you.

80. You were in my dreams last night.

81. Fuck me

82. Don't stop

83. 8====D

84. Faster

85. I'm almost there

86. Use your sperminator on me.

87. Use that dick of yours

88. I love it when I get you hard.

89. You are so hot.

90. Your muscles are bulging

91. I want that dick in me now

92. Your penis makes me wet.

93. I want to play with your balls.

94. Tell me how bad you want me

95. Oh you have me soaking wet, come in me and play

96. Be my little secret.

97. Make me cum in every room.

98. You got me wishing I knew you earlier.

99. Choke me with that cock of yours

100. I'm gagging on you, please don't stop.

BDSM Positions:

The Beginner's Guide to BDSM

Introduction

I want to thank you and congratulate you for downloading the book, *BDSM Positions: The Beginner's Guide to BDSM*. Downloading this book is the first step to exploring a facet of human sexuality that statistically speaking you and your partner will both enjoy at least to a mild degree. BDSM is a complex and potentially dangerous milieu of intersecting practices and kinks but it never has to evolve beyond what you and your partner are comfortable with.

This book contains proven steps and strategies on how to take BDSM experimentation one step at a time, with an emphasis on never doing more than what you and your partner are safe and comfortable exploring. The basics of BDSM can be extremely stimulating and fulfilling for most partners without ever stepping outside the bounds of mild restriction and sensation play.

Cautiously explore the following chapters and see what within piques your interest or seems as though it may pique your partner's. Remember, there is nothing wrong with a little experimentation and you won't know what you both will like until you try.

Thanks again for downloading this book, I hope you enjoy it!

Chapter 1: Defining the Rules

When the phrase BDSM comes up in conversation, many people immediately think of the extreme, leather, chains, ball gags and more than likely, plenty of pain. Unfortunately for those who never have the opportunity to experience it first hand, BDSM has come to by synonymous with only the most extreme practices which fall under the moniker when in reality BDSM encompasses a wide array of activities which run the gamut from pleasurable to painful.

For starters, lets define BDSM to allow for a better understanding of what is involved. BDSM stands for bondage, dominance, sadism and masochism. When taken as a whole BDSM can be broadly described as being dominated, restrained or otherwise made to submit to the whims of your partner. While some people take it to the next level by experiencing pleasure while either giving or receiving pain, you can have a full and adventurous time in the world of BDSM without experiencing either. As it should be with any type of sexual experience, the experiences you have dabbling with BDSM are completely and totally within your control at all times, it should never be about experiencing pleasure at the expense of your partner.

Establish Ground Rules
When first beginning to experience with BDSM it is important that you and you partner discuss in detail what is and what is not acceptable. A good first step would to be to each write out a list of things that are and are not acceptable in any sexual situation. It is important that this not be done in the heat of the moment as that can lead to a situation where a partner feels pressured into doing something that they otherwise might not be comfortable with.

When deciding on what is and is not acceptable, you should at least consider the following list of options and know how you partner feels about them.
- **How do you feel about being tied up?** This is perhaps the most basic tenant of BDSM as the loss of control can be considered an aphrodisiac to many people. Do you

prefer to just have your legs or arms tied but not both? Let your partner know. If you have never been restrained before perhaps it is best to simulate the scenario before starting for real.

- **What do you like to have done to you while you are restrained?** The degree of sexual stimulation a person enjoys while being restrained varies from person to person, some people only like to be restrained during foreplay while others prefer to be restrained during intercourse, either is fine, as is neither, as long as you and your partner are both happy.
- **What sensations do you enjoy the most?** Another core tenant of BDSM is an oscillation of sensations applied, generally while one of the partners is restrained. As such it is important to know what sensations your partner enjoys but also which they do not. Nothing ruins the mood faster than the application of stimulation that you absolutely hate.
- **Anything else that makes you uncomfortable.** If there are situations that could occur while experimenting with BDSM that you feel are absolutely off limits such as your partner leaving the room while you are bound for example should be explicitly stated beforehand. Proper planning is key to all partners having a good time.

Play safe

When experimenting with the BDSM community there are two important safety acronyms to keep in mind. RACK (risk aware consensual kink) and SSC (safe, sane, consensual). Taken together they mean that any activity you engage in should always be consensual, risky activities should never be attempted while any partner is not of sound mind and that safety should always be a number one priority.

To ensure that safety remains a top priority in any form of BDSM play it is important to have a mutually agreed upon safe word which can be used to put a stop to whatever is going on at any time. This word should be something that would not normally come up during the act such as banana or purple octopus. While this can seem like a lot of effort to put into sex without actually having any sex, the foundation of a successful BDSM relationship is a firm set of ground rules and the mutual trust to always follow them.

Start out slow

Studies show that far more people experiment with some aspect of BDSM than people think. In fact, close to 70 percent of the population can be said to have explored the idea in some detail in their sexual lifetimes. Consider this, pinning your partner's arms, spanking or blindfolding can all be considered a form of bondage. The reason that some people find the lack of control so arousing is that they find it stimulates their other senses when one is impaired.

The first thing to consider when deciding to be restrained is how you and your partner are comfortable being dressed. If your partner is intrigue by the idea of BDSM but scared at the practice, getting them used to the idea by restraining them while clothed can be a good place to start.

Blindfolding your partner will cause them to experience every sound more vividly and to use their imagination to discover what you will do to them. Likewise, restraining your partner will heighten all sense of touch. Starting off with restraints that close with Velcro is a great idea as it will give your partner the sensation of being restrained without forcing them to give up all forms of control at once. This can lead to handcuffs or even door jam or hog-tie restraints but as always it is about only doing what the other person is comfortable with.

For those who prefer to work up to even Velcro restraints, a dog collar and leash can be a good place to start. This will allow both partners to get comfortable with the idea of restricted movement without actually doing that much to restrict their movement. If you are working up to being restrained to a bed, try a dog collar, leash and a set of Velcro handcuffs.

By combining a blindfold with some form of restraints any other sensory input will be heightened to the extreme. In these situations, the subconscious tries to convince the conscious mind that the situation it finds itself in is dangerous which stimulates the senses even more. Proceed to this level cautiously however as the experience can easily overwhelm novice partners.

Chapter 2: Start with a Feather

Once all of the specifics have been discussed beforehand, the best way to begin an introductory BDSM experience is to begin by using a feather. For the remainder of this book the person who is being restrained will be referred to as the **submissive** while the other partner will be referred as the **dominant.** What many people find so enjoyable about the BDSM experience is that those in the role of submissive have no control over the sexual pleasure they are receiving while dominant partners enjoy being the gatekeeper of their partner's pleasure.

This in turn allows the dominant to experiment with numerous erotic sensations from heat, to ice, to feathers, fabrics, fingers and toys. Starting with feathers or silk is a good way to ease your partner into a BDSM experience. They excite, tickle and arouse the skin with just the simplest touch. Start by restraining your partner lightly and running the soft item around their erogenous zones, experiment and see what you both enjoy the most. As previously discussed, BDSM experiences do not need to include situations when the dominant violates the submissive while they are restrained. Finding the right mix of stimuli to bring your partner to the absolute heights of pleasure should be a fun sexual adventure for you both.

Try your tongue
While your partner is restrained, try experimenting with the pleasure you can provide with just your tongue alone. Experiment with your partner's neck, mouth, face, chest and other erogenous zones. If the submissive is both restrained and blindfolded the variety of sensations available from a combination of sucking, licking and kissing will drive your partner wild. Tease with quick flicks of the tongue, blow gently on their most sensitive areas or lightly bite them with your

teeth. Oral sex as part of the BDSM experience can be completely different experience than when done in a non-BDSM situations. The dominant will completely control the experience as the submissive is helpless to influence their own orgasm. Those looking to enhance the experience further can look into a variety of products including warming gels, ice or even Altoids.

Move on to toys
Contrary to popular conceptions, dominants take pleasure in providing pleasure to their partners, the fact that this pleasure can be derived from pain is irrelevant. After you and your partner have experimented with the pleasure derived from using your mouth and soft things such as silk scarves or feathers, you might be ready to try something a little more intense. When a submissive is both restrained and blindfolded the noise that many sex toys make can be as stimulating as the pleasure it provides. Starting with a simple vibrator will allow the dominant to tease all of their partner's erogenous zones whether that partner is male or female. Adding warming gels or massage oils in tandem can increase your partner's sensations even further.

Depending on what you and your partner have discussed prior to beginning to experiment in the realm of BDSM teasing with sex toys can be extended to full on penetration. Remember, do not take this step without first discussing it with your partner as some people do not like to be penetrated while restrained. With the level of consent determined it is always important to have lubrication handy before moving on to insertion. The type of toy can vastly affect the type of stimulation it provides. If you and you partner are experimenting with this type of play for the first time it is best to start with several different low cost toys, see which provide the most pleasure and then go from there.

Taking it to the next level

If you and your partner have experimented with a variety of BDSM foreplay scenarios and are both comfortable taking it to the next level, then participating in consensual restrained sex is the next erotic step. Moving on to penetrative sex with restraints allows the dominant to be in full control of the coitus while the submissive once more is solely at their whim to as to the pleasure provided.

If you and your partner are interested in taking things up a notch in another way, it may be time to experiment to determine if a little bit of pain can lead to a whole lot more pleasure. Spanking and biting cause excess blood to flow to the affected area which then increases the stimulation felt in the affected area. Many people enjoy having their nipples pinched lightly or a restrained spanking and when experimenting in this arena this is the best place to start. The most important thing is to start off slowly and build the sensations from there and experimenting with different blends of pleasure and pain. Everyone has a different pain threshold which is why this step should be explored with extreme caution.

Suggested Items
The following items can be considered essentially for anyone investigating the BDSM experience.

Rope: Statistically speaking most people have some bit of rope lying around that could, in a pinch, be used to restrain a submissive. This is a mindset that many budding BDSM enthusiasts find themselves in but in reality, the type of rope matters. Most rope is to rough or hard to restrain a person without rubbing the skin raw, especially if you plan on having penetrative sex while restrained. Using the wrong rope can end a BDSM experience before it fully begins so do yourself a favor and purchase bondage rope, it will be designed not leave marks, be machine washable and most importantly be nice and soft when it comes in contact with skin. Nylon rope available at most hardware stores is generally considered the next best thing.

Handcuffs: Another BDSM staple, handcuffs provide less readily available variety than rope and should be considered if your partner does not like their legs to be restrained. These days, handcuffs come in three major varieties.

- *Traditional metal handcuffs* are cheap, easy to use and as a bonus can easily add a bit of roleplay to the proceedings. The biggest downside to these cuffs is their lack of padding, which may or may not be an issue depending on the submissive's pain tolerance. Non-official versions also tend to break easily.
- *Padded handcuffs:* When first starting out experimenting with BDSM scenarios these are most likely the cuffs you will want to try first. They are much thicker than traditional cuffs so they will not leave marks and they are generally sealed using Velcro so a new submissive won't have anything to worry about. They tend to be more expensive than metal cuffs, though not by much. When looking for padded cuffs be sure to look online at customer reviews to ensure that what you pick will be up to the challenge.
- *Bondage Tape:* While not a pair of handcuffs per se, bondage tape is a relatively new product which promises to only stick to itself and not your hair or your skin. It is as easy to remove as it is to put on and, even better, its reusable. This product is cheap, inconspicuous and can be used for more than just cuffs. For beginning BDSM enthusiasts this is most likely the best bet.

Blindfold

While it may seem that there are many items which can be used in place of a blindfold, few do the job as well as an item designed for the task. A quality blindfold will prevent all light from getting through, while still remaining comfortable for the submissive and easy to put on and remove. Dealing with a substitute can be difficult as well as time consuming and can easily ruin the mood. Do yourself a favor and pick up a proper blindfold, you can generally find them sold as sleep masks at most pharmacies for around $20.

Household Items
When beginning your BDSM adventure there are several common household items that can be used to enhance the experience so you and your partner can determine what you enjoy without putting a lot of money down of items you may or may not use.

- *Pastry brush:* A common pastry brush can be used in place of a feather to provide an introduction to what is broadly referred to as "sensation play"
- *Spatula:* If you or your partner are interested in investigating your feelings on spanking further then a spatula will be your best bet. Silicone spatulas work best for beginners. Wooden or metal spatulas should be worked up to. Remember, never use silicone based lube on any silicone items as it will ruin them.
- *Snake Bite Kit:* While seemingly both innocuous and incredibly un-sexy most snake bites kits tend to come with a pair of suction cups that are ideal when experimenting with nipple play before moving on to more robust options such as clips or clamps.

Chapter 3: Starter Positions

After you and your partner have experimented with the basic aspects of BDSM the following list and description of various bondage positions can help you take the experience to the next level. As with everything else concerning BDSM it is important to discuss what you and your partner are comfortable with before proceeding.

Ball Tie: The Ball Tie is a position in which the goal is to place the submissive into a position resembling a ball. The legs should be secured in such a way that the thighs press against the chest. The hands can be restrained either in front of or behind the back. The position can be considered both stringent and stimulating while still remaining comfortable.

Breast Bondage: This technique involves tying a woman in such a way that they accentuate the breasts, and is more about the look than any restrictive effect. This form of restraint can be performed with clothes or without. The most basic form involves placing a rope around the torso slightly above the breasts then adding a second rope tied just bellowed them. Finally, a third roped is then looped over the shoulders to lie between the breasts so it can be drawn over the other ropes to hold them tightly together.

Crotch Rope: This technique ties a rope around a woman's waist in such a way that the rope passes between the labia for the purpose of applying stimulating pleasure to the region. Specific forms of this technique can be adapted to apply to men as well. In general, the rope slips between the labia majora or past the vulva cleft. Depending on the fashion in which the knots are tied it can also apply pressure to the clitoris or anus depending. The rope is typically attached above the hips and draped across the genitals before being tied off and slipped down and around to connect back to its source on the other side.

Frog Tie: This technique binds a person's legs in such a way that their legs are held so that the feet are near the inner-thighs. Each ankle is restrained to its adjacent thigh and the arms are then placed behind the back as each arm is connected to the thigh as well. This position allows for a vulnerable but not completely immobile restraint. For a more advanced form of this technique bind the submissive's wrists to their opposite ankles for a more stringent restraint.

Head Bondage: This type of bondage technique can be broken down into two categories. The first involves the use of a bondage hood, which may include a blindfold as well as a gag as well as a heavy collar or other attachment points for more involved BDSM experiences. It may also refer to the use of rope or a similar item to restrict head movement. A head harness, perhaps more so than other techniques discussed previously creates more of a sense of objectification and helplessness in the submissive and should be first performed in a situation where the submissive can be easily removed if needed.

Hog Tie: This technique involves binding the submissive's wrists and ankles before fastening both sets of extremities behind the back while they are lying face down. The legs are then bent at the knees and connected to a restraint which run the length of the body, holding them up in the air. When attempting this position, it is important to know that it places a large amount of pressure on the abdomen which in turn can make it difficult for the submissive to breathe. As such it is very important to ensure that the submissive can breathe freely at all stages of this form of restraint.

Spread Eagle Tie: This technique involves restraining the submissive in such a way that they are readily in a position to encourage sexual stimulation. This technique involves securing the submissive to three or four separate points depending on if an X or Y spread eagle is desired. This position is popularly used with a Saint Andrews Cross but a sturdy bedframe will work just as well. For a Y spread eagle simple connect the submissive's hands together above their head instead of separately. A spread eagle can be performed with either the submissive face up or face down although the face down method inherently produces risks of asphyxiation.

Over-arm Tie: The over-arm technique is a positon whereby the submissive's arms are restrained behind their head by ropes or other types of restraints which are connected to their ankles. The over-arm tie is another form of tie that is often used as much for the aesthetic affect as it is to restrict movement and as such it is often combined with additional bondage techniques including the crotch rope or a modified version of the frog tie. If you and your partner are looking for something a little more restrictive it can easily be combined with the hog tie or the shrimp tie.

Reverse Prayer: This technique requires a the submissive's arms to be bound behind them in the opposite position they would be in if they folded their arms in prayer. To enact this position, the submissive must place their hands between their shoulders while keeping the fingers of both hands extended and their palms touching. The wrists are then bound together with a series of restrains before a rope is looped around the chest and drawn over the wrists to hold them in place. This technique is uncomfortable for many people and can lead to cramps over time. When attempting this position, it is important not to overdo it so that the submissive's elbows are touching as this can easily lead to dislocation.

Rope Harness: This technique involves binding the submissive in a complex web of restraints to hold them up completely. This technique requires between 30 and 45 feet of rope to try and will require much practice to do correctly. Start by tying a bowline knot around one leg. Take the long end of the rope and tie another bowline knot around the other leg. Wrap the remaining length of rope around the back and through the crotch area to form a diamond shape. Continue following the same basic pattern as you move up the body. This technique can be more or less restrictive depending on if you wrap the arms or wrap the rope under the arms.

Shrimp Tie: This technique first gained popularity in Japan more than 300 years ago as a means of interrogation and torture, as such, which this form of bondage can be great in short doses, a prolonged session can cause intense discomfort. To begin, the submissive sits with their legs crossed and their hands behind their back. Begin by binding the ankles together before connecting that restraint to one that is looped around the submissive's neck (with plenty of breathing room) which is then attached to the ankles. The arms are then bound behind the back and that restraint is also connected to the main restraint.

Suspension bondage: As the name implies, this technique involves hanging the submissive from a single or several overhead suspension points. The type of suspension can be either horizontal or vertical, partial or complete, but always carries a higher level of risk than the techniques discussed above. The main goal in suspension activities is to create an even greater sense of restraint and vulnerability in the submissive as the act of trying to free themselves becomes more inherently dangerous. Vertical suspension is generally achieved by lifting the submissive from the ground by their wrists, horizontal suspension is generally achieved by utilizing a hog tie position and inverted suspension in achieved by lifting the submissive from the ground using their legs. These positions can easily restrict the submissive's airway if not done properly and extreme caution should always be used for the submissive's safety.

Strappado Bondage: This term is used to describe a technique in which the submissive's arms are bound behind their back then attached to a suspension point above. The submissive's legs can either be secured to one another or to another point on the ground. The submissive's arms are then elevated in such a way that they are required to bend forward. The term strappado comes from a form of torture still used in some countries to this day. This form of bondage must be practiced carefully as it can easily cause permanent damage to the submissive's arms and shoulder's if jerked to forcefully.

Japanese bondage: Called Kinbaku which means "the beauty of tight binding" this technique involves binding the submissive's buttocks in an erotically attractive pattern. This type of bondage can include binding the wrists either together or separate, binding the hands either in front of or behind the back, using a diamond pattern and binding while either standing or suspended. Many of the techniques in Kinbaku can be complicated and thus open to a higher degree of risk and should only be explored further when both you and your partner feel the need for advanced techniques.

Classic Damsel: So named for the way the submissive lays, the elbows are tied together so they are touching behind the back, the wrists are connected together and the legs are restrained together below the knees as well as the ankles.

Legs Up Ball Tie: This is a variation on the classic ball tie. You start by binding the submissive's waste and thighs together, you then bind the arms to the ankles so both are straight out. One or both sets of restraints will need to be attached to a secure point above her head.

Tiptoe crotch rope spreader bar strappado: In this position the ankles are connected to a spreader bar. The submissive is then asked to stand on tiptoe while their elbows are bound together behind the back. The crotch rope is primarily used as decoration and additional stimulation.

Yoke Positon: This position simulates the barnyard implement of the same name and requires a sturdy pole as well as rope. When attaching a pole at neck height be very careful to not restrict the breathing. Place the pole on the back of the neck and secure the arms to it before securing the neck.

Crab Position: In this position the submissive sits with their back bent forward so their hands reach their feet. The arms are then bound to the legs at the wrist and again at the elbow. The submissive then leans back and balances on their buttocks.

Chair Position: This position is perfect for restraining a submissive over a piece of furniture. Have the submissive bend over the chair and restrain them the way you would with a ball tie. Then bind them to the chair above the elbow and above the knee. The hands and feet can also be bound.

Waitress Position: The term "waitress" refers to any position where the hands are restrained in front of the body while the elbows are restrained behind. The severity of the position desired determines at what point the elbows are bound though right above the elbow is considered standard.

Double V: In this position the submissive's arms are restrained together with each hand gripping the opposite shoulder. The hands are tied to the upper arm and bound together at the elbow as well. The submissive sits with their legs folded and a rope binds the feet and attaches to the arms.

The Offering: In this position the submissive's hands are bound together overhead while the legs are held apart either side to side or in a lunging pose. Remember when the arms are bound above the head always ensure that the submissive can breathe easily. Use caution.

Caterpillar: Any position that involves wrapping the submissive completely in rope can be referred to as a caterpillar. Similar to a rope web though more elaborate it can be considered mainly decorative though due to its nature it does make an effective leg binding option. Typically, the rope runs the length of the body while the hands are restrained above the head.

Bottoms Up: In this position the submissive is placed in a crotch rope which is attached to a point overhead. The submissive kneels on their hands and knees and their feet and hands are then bound together.

Olympic Mascot: In this position the submissive is made to bend over and touch their toes. They are then fitted with a crotch rope attached to a point overhead. Their feet and hands are each bound separately before finally being connected with together by a short length of rope.

Box Tie Position: This position is used in many more elaborate positions as well. In it the submissive places their arms behind their back so each hand is grabbing the opposite arm above the elbow. The wrists are then bound together and connected to a restraint which wraps around the front of the body both above and below the breasts.

Hooplah: In this position the submissive first places their arms behind their back the arms are then bound by wrapping them repeatedly from wrist to above the shoulder. A second restraint is then looped around the submissive's neck and above and below the wrists before connecting around the back to the wrists.

The Stardust: In this position the submissive places their hands behind their back so that one hand lays on each buttocks. Restraints are then wrapped around the body including the hands at the hips, and the stomach and those two are connected together. Then again above and below the wrists which are then also connected together. The two sections are then connected together.

Diving Springboard: In this position the submissive starts on the ground with their legs sticking up in the air. The legs are bound together between the knee and the calf before binding the ankles together. The wrists are then bound together and connected to the ankles. The ankles are then connected to a point above the head.

Conclusion

Thank you again for downloading this book! I hope it was able to help you to begin to explore the complex and erotic world of BDSM experimentation. Remember, when first starting out it is important to discuss the specifics in detail with your partner and to always perform BDSM practices responsibly by considering RACK and SCC before committing to anything. Finally, always be aware of which types of activities need to be practiced with extra caution, nothing will ruin the mood faster than having to call 911 because your partner nearly asphyxiated because you hog-tied them improperly.

The next step is to put down this book already and find a partner you feel comfortable discussing the erotic possibilities that BDSM can provide, your more fulfilling sex life will thank you.

Finally, if you enjoyed this book, then I'd like to ask you for a favor, would you be kind enough to leave a review for this book on Amazon? It'd be greatly appreciated!

Printed in Great Britain
by Amazon